One Tech **Action**

One Tech

Action

A quick-and-easy guide to getting started
using productivity apps and websites
for busy professionals

Crystal WashingtonZ

Author Portrait: CJ Martin, www.rmfoto.com
Cover Design: Jesus Cordero
Book Design: Mark Gelotte, www.markgelotte.com

ISBN: 0-9892144-1-9

Library of Congress Control Number: 2016917087

1. Social media 2. Mobile apps 3. iPhone (Smartphone)—Mobile apps
4. Work-life balance 5. Job-hunting 6. Personal and professional development
7. Success 8. Productivity 9. Browsers (Computer programs)

ATTENTION CORPORATIONS, PROFESSIONAL ASSOCIATIONS AND ORGANIZATIONS:
McCarthy House Press books are available at special quantity discounts for use in corporate trainings, sales promotions, or as conference materials. For more information, please contact Sales, McCarthy House Press, 448 W 19th Street #327, Houston, TX 77008, (713) 383-9351.

The author has also written: *The Social Media Why: A Busy Professional's Practical Guide to Using Social Media Including LinkedIn, Facebook, Twitter, YouTube, Pinterest, Google+ and Blogs for Business*
For information on workshops and keynote speeches, or to learn more about social media and mobile marketing, please visit www.crystalwashington.com.

For Bralyn, Mekhi, Erick, Shawn, Elijah,
and all those yet to come.

Contents

PREFACE ix

MY STORY xiii

HOW TO READ THIS BOOK xvii

SECTION 1: **THE DIGITAL SHIFT**. 1

How Did We Get Here? 3
Technology Overload. 6
Make It Work for You. 10

SECTION 2: **ALL ABOUT APPS**. 15

Appsolutely Fabulous! 17
   Do I Have Enough Space for Apps? 22
   Where to Get Apps 23
   Finding Apps on iOS. 24
   Finding Apps on Android. 25
Stay Safe 26
   What the Experts Say 26
   Five Tips for Staying Safe 34
Meet the Apps. 36

SECTION 3: **INTELLIGENT ASSISTANTS, EXTENSIONS, AND MORE** . . .65

Intelligent Assistants 66
Browser Extensions 70
Web Services 75

SECTION 4: **TAKE ONE SIMPLE TECH ACTION** 79

Get Comfortable with Your Intelligent Assistant 81
Adjust Your Settings 86
Start Taking One Tech Action! 87
    Connect with Friends and Family 87
    Find a Job 94
    Build Better Business Connections 101
    Get Clients 110
    Improve/Organize Home Life 118
    Personal Development 123
    Plan and Enjoy Free Time 127
    Self-Care in the Technology Age 130
    Enjoy a Digital Detox 131
    Start a Smartphone Diet 132
    Set Boundaries 133
    Finding It Hard to Power Off? 135
    Putting It All Together 136

EASY REFERENCE APPS CHART 137

EASY REFERENCE BROWSER EXTENSION CHART 139

ADDITIONAL RESOURCES 140
    Blogs and Websites 140
    Books 141

GLOSSARY 142

ACKNOWLEDGEMENTS 152

ABOUT THE AUTHOR 154

Preface

If you're like most people, you were brought up with a few myths. One of the first legends we were introduced to as children was that of Santa Claus, which brought a magical time into our young lives. Another one would probably be Big Foot. Has anyone ever actually seen a nongrainy picture of that guy? Either he doesn't exist or he is nature's first naturally pixelated animal. Perhaps, the most heinous myth of all is the myth of **work-life balance**. I hate to be the bearer of bad news, but—**it doesn't exist**, it is an unachievable goal. Have you ever known anyone claiming they had achieved this concept who was not paid to pontificate on the subject?

Most of us are overloaded and don't have enough hours in the day to finish everything we need to complete. All the prioritizing in the world won't fix that problem. The only viable option we have is to push things off of our plates! That's where technology comes into play!

In addition to finding that perfect time allotment between our professional and personal lives, the line separating our home and work time is both fuzzy and curvy—but don't tell my geometry teacher I suggested a line could be curvy—often having no clear demarcation. When we feel as though we're not checking items off our to-do list at home, it becomes challenging to concentrate on completing tasks at work. And vice-versa when projects at the office are not properly executed, we have difficulty being attentive in our home lives.

There is a solution—it's called technology. Just as the invention of the washing machine and car saved our grandparents time, so can mobile-device technology, specifically apps, save us time. This book provides practical solutions that will allow you to increase your efficiency at home, work, and all the places in-between.

I'm sure you're well aware of the digital revolution and how our lives have become permeated with technology—smartphones, computers, laptops, wearable devices, apps, extensions, websites, smart appliances, the Internet of Things, and so much more! How are normal people—real people whose full-time job is not keeping up with technology—supposed to stay up-to-date on all of these things?

Luckily, you don't need the vast majority of technology that is out there. As with all good things—e.g., medication—overuse and overdependence creates, rather than solves problems. Overuse of technology weakens our ability to communicate, build relationships, and even sleep! However, if we're smart, we use things like apps in ways that make us more productive, freeing us to spend more time on achieving our goals and spending more precious moments with loved ones.

Do you want to become an app expert—understand their history, how they work, and how to develop them? If so, do not buy this book; it is not for you. However, if you're a busy professional of any age who wants to begin incorporating apps and web browser extensions into your everyday life to become more efficient and effective, this is the book for you. When you are done, you will not be a specialist, but you will be immediately more proficient.

Apps and extensions are not magic; they are only as good as their user. If you make the time to implement some of the suggestions in this book, you will see positive changes. If you don't make the time, you will never know how much easier life could be.

My goal is to present a buffet of "healthy" technology options for you to choose from, as well as give you the plate and serving utensils so you can start eating immediately. It's an honor to have the opportunity to serve you and demonstrate how you can cut out the busy work and other energy-sapping boondoggles that are stealing your attention away from the things that really matter to you.

My Story

I'll start off by admitting I am an afro-puff-wearing, earthy tech-nerd from Generation Y, also called the Millennial Generation. What makes me unique is that I'm a Gen Y with a dash of Gen X cynicism and Baby Boomer sensibility. While I value advancement and crave technology, I tend to think in terms of practical applications—such as "How does a new piece of technology make life easier?" or "How is this a better use of my time than that?" Social media enabled me to quit my job in corporate America to start a marketing firm from my home. Sites like LinkedIn, Facebook, YouTube, and Twitter empowered me to grow my clients' businesses. I expanded my network of contacts, met amazing and inspiring people, and helped business owners and professionals use social media to find jobs, increase sales, and attract opportunities. I've been blessed to travel not only throughout the United States, but even to Africa and Europe as a speaker. I'm basically paid to do the one thing my parents tried to get me to stop doing for the first eighteen years of my life—talk.

Unlike most of my peers, I have a strong desire to balance technology and the "real world." If you were to run into me, you would be able to pick me out pretty easily, and not only because I have a bright red afro puff. In a group with my friends or family, I am likely the only one **not** on a mobile device. I only want to use technology as long as it makes me more efficient, effective, and connected. Once it starts taking away from family time or connecting with friends or giving my clients my full attention, I know it's time to put it away.

The ability to connect and foster relationships is why I enjoy technology so much. Before it was popular to use social networks for business, I was in awe of the fact that in a matter of seconds, I could connect with hundreds of people. Not only that, I could get to know them and build relationships. It may not seem like a big deal now, but it definitely was back then.

In 2013, I wrote the book *The Social Media Why: A Busy Professional's Practical Guide to Using Social Media Including LinkedIn, Facebook, Twitter, YouTube, Pinterest, Google+ and Blogs for Business.* The book explained social media in plain English for everyday people, who just wanted to understand the practical applications. Clients, audience members, and people from all over the world commented on how easy the book was to understand and how, for the first time, many of them felt knowledgeable and up-to-date on social media.

Since then, with the rise of the sharing economy—with apps such as Uber and Postmates—and the saturation of our minds with "new" technology, I've come to understand that many of us are not taking full advantage of productivity opportunities with these apps.

Prior to penning (oops, I mean typing; Gen Y—remember?) this book, I surveyed over 700 busy professionals like yourself. When asked to share the biggest challenge they face in incorporating technology into their everyday lives, the number one answer from over 60% of the respondents was lack of time. The question was an open-ended one, meaning they were not given a list of choices, yet most came up with the same response. At the same time, the vast majority of those surveyed felt they were falling behind and wanted to stay abreast of useful technology.

So, I drove to a home in the Texas Hill Country for a few days to cordon myself off from technology in order to write another book on technology—specifically on productivity apps and extensions—that anyone could understand. As a result, I sit here writing in a mighty Texas heat wave with my crimson afro blowing in a strong wind while a very nosy and rude deer stares at me from across the street.

What follows in the next few pages is my sincere effort to assist everyday people in incorporating technology into their lives to increase efficacy. As you review this book, please keep in mind that it is your choice which actions to take. Please do not feel pressured to incorporate every or even most items suggested. Use what will work for you and leave the rest!

Whatever tools you decide to use, know that in reading this book and being open to learning about technology, you are taking a huge step toward accomplishing your goals. I wish you continued blessings in your journey!

Crystal Washington
Wimberly, TX
2016

How to Read This Book

This book was written for you, the busy professional. Keeping up with new apps, extensions, and websites can be daunting, if not just plain overwhelming. It's impossible to be knowledgeable of all of them. The good news is you don't need to incorporate all the latest technology into your life. One small action daily or weekly is enough for you to see positive results. This book, more of a what-to-do rather than a how-to, was written to help you incorporate simple, easy-to-implement tech fixes to make you more efficient, effective, and connected.

There are numerous ways to read this book. If you are unfamiliar with app terms, I suggest you read the glossary first. If you are unsure of the value of apps or extensions, I encourage you to read through the entire book to gain a solid understanding of their practical applications. However, if you are just curious about a single tool, feel free to skip to Section 2 or 3.

If you find that you become overwhelmed with too many options, skip through to Section 4 where you can start taking action, based on your goals. As you make selections, read the glossary for an explanation of the services recommended.

Not all of the resources in this book will be of interest or even apply to you. Feel free to cherry-pick and use just those items that will help you get ahead. No matter how you choose to read this resource or what items you decide to implement, it is my genuine intention that the information presented in this book serves you and the greater good.

Apps, social networks, and extensions are constantly changing, but I've worked hard to ensure the information presented in this book is accurate as of the time of publication.

One Tech
Action

Section 1: **The Digital Shift**

How Did We Get Here?

So how did we get here? The short answer—technology advancements are happening at exponential rates! The first computer, completed in 1946, occupied nearly 1800 square feet of space and weighed a whopping 50 tons!

The Motorola DynaTAC 8000X was the first commercially available cell phone, retailing at just below 4000 USD. First marketed in 1983, it was 13 x 1.75 x 3.5 inches in dimension, weighed about 2.5 pounds, and featured a then impressive thirty-minute talk time.

Compare these inventions to today's iPhone, over a million times more powerful than either predecessor, and it fits into the palm of your hand and weighs between *4–6 ounces*.

Here's a fun activity that will change how you think about your smartphone. Write down all of the physical—tangible—items the smartphone has replaced. For example, the Walkman or your bank would be good answers because it could be argued that Spotify and banking apps have replaced them, respectively.

List as many as you'd like or set a timer for five minutes and see how many you can list.

_____

_____

_____

_____

_____

_____

_____

I hope you completed the above activity. If so, you're likely blown away by how powerful the little smartphone is—after all, it's a powerful computer that travels along with you in your pocket. I set a timer for five minutes to see how many tangible items I could list, and I came up with sixty-five! A few of my answers were books, scanner, level (for hanging pictures), credit card, and rolodex.

With the creation of the Internet and, eventually, the rise of social media (the natural successor of chat rooms), people saw the opportunity to connect with friends and family in new ways. Ultimately, the reach expanded with people using the networks to go beyond their circles: to create brands, hire employees, follow celebrities, and contact people all over the world with whom they have no local or common connections.

The increase in usage of social media encouraged advancements in smartphones as more and more users were accessing networks from phones versus computers.

Meanwhile, the time consumers spent on mobile devices was on the rise. Companies competed to create better smartphone experiences. As a result, the app was born!

The creation and adoption of apps completely shifted how we interacted with our phones. Now phones were no longer simply for talking, texting, or taking pictures. Your phone can now give directions, check in to your flights, cash checks, order groceries, and so much more.

When we look at how our teens often misuse technology and how addicted some of our friends appear to be, it's easy to see how someone could be apprehensive about this new world. It can be an overwhelming experience, living in the digital age when much of our population uses text talk on resumes, rather than communicating in full sentences, and emojis (those little faces and objects that are included in messaging/texting) in supposedly professional emails. Rest assured, the sky is not falling. You and I will adapt, like we've been doing our entire lives. While it is not unusual to see people abusing money, buying things that actually hurt their bodies and their minds, the answer is not to forgo money. We can heed their example and use it as a warning to spend money on healthful things—nourishing food, smart investments, and quality time with family. So, the next time one of your time-wasting friends, who's always wrapped up in her phone, says you have to try this new app or game because it's so much fun, I need you to look at him or her like the drug dealer that they are and just say no!

Choose to spend your technology currency wisely in ways that enrich your life.

Technology Overload

This chapter came dangerously close to being named "My Brain Is on Fire—Help Me!" The world has changed dramatically in a relatively small amount of time. It appears that gone are the days of most families enjoying uninterrupted family time without intrusive smartphones perched in everyone's hands. Also disappearing is our ability to offer each other what one of my mentors, Hitaji Aziz, calls "delighted attention," which is simply being with someone and gifting them with our full attention. It has also become challenging to focus on and take care of oneself. Luckily, there are solutions for that too, which will be discussed further in Chapter 13, Self-Care in the Technology Age.

Nearly every audience member I've ever polled has shared that they're overwhelmed and feel like they're behind when it comes to using mobile technology. How do we find time to research apps, social media, and smart devices when we barely have enough time to take care of all of our commitments at work and at home? The answer is little-by-little—in bite-sized chunks.

Additionally, what no one seems to discuss is the fact that technology can be scary at times due to fear of making mistakes, constant updates, and valid security concerns. Boomers and Traditionalists were brought up with the belief that if you're going to do something, do it right the first time! Making a mistake, which will erase something important or cause a computer to shut down or make a smartphone freeze up, is a real fear for many highly intelligent people. Because of this, too many Boomers and Traditionalists believe young people are naturally more adept with technology. This is not so! Millennials and Xers are just used to adapting and tend to embrace the fact that mistakes will happen—but you can recover and learn from them.

I'm an old Millennial; meaning I was born just a few months shy of being a Gen Xer. In my lifetime, I've used records, eight-tracks, cassette tapes, CDs, MP3s, and Spotify. My generation is used to adapting because technology has shifted rapidly over our entire lives. When I was a small child, it was not standard for everyone to have a computer in the home. However, certainly by the time I was in high school and in college, almost every family in my neighborhood owned a computer.

Younger people know that a part of learning is making mistakes. If you only knew how many times I've lost files or messed something up, you'd likely be shocked. That's part of the learning process, and it's going to happen. The good thing is that, with a level head, most mistakes can be fixed and those that can't don't spell the end of the world. Even with those mistakes, leveraging social media and apps has made my life far more efficient than it would have been without them. As long as you have solid judgment, you'll be fine. While it can be hard to come back from posting compromising pictures of yourself on the web (which I am certain you will not do), it is far easier to rebound from deleting a note on OneNote. Give yourself permission to learn and mess some things up!

In fact, it's been my experience that most mistakes can be fixed with a quick trip to Google or YouTube where you can type in your problem and find an answer. There are thousands of conversation threads on the web where people have likely already found a solution for your error message, app freezing, nonworking laptop touchpad, etc.

The first step is to have a shift in thinking. Benjamin Franklin once said, "An ounce of prevention is worth a pound of cure." We have to make the time. Some of the action items I suggest in this book will take you five minutes to set up, but will save you one to two hours per week.

Using technology is a great deal like investing: invest a little now for a larger payout later. Luckily, technology's payoff is typically much faster. Also, like investing, knowing what you're doing before you invest resources is a key component. I have a secret to tell you. Lean in...most of your seemingly techie family and friends really aren't getting any positive, measurable results using smart devices and the web. They're using the resources, but are often wasting time. You're going to learn how to avoid falling into the technology time warp.

The second step is to simply commit to doing the work! Saying you don't have ten minutes a week to invest in learning or implementing a productivity tool is akin to stating that you don't have ten minutes to transfer money into an investment that is guaranteed to give you an annual return of 15% per year. It's insane! Make the time.

Make It Work for You

Incorporating technology into your everyday life is akin to planting seeds in a garden, where you invest time now in order to enjoy delicious fresh vegetables later. Fortunately, leveraging technology is much easier than gardening, and I should know as I've done both. Not even Tim Burton could have imagined the massively huge and terrifying bugs Texas awarded me in return for my laboring in the dirt.

Some of the action items in this book will be a matter of you downloading new apps or incorporating other new items. Conversely, you'll find recommendations to remove popular apps in order to improve your efficiency by minimizing those time-sucks, which deplete your energies.

Have you ever stopped to really think about all of the things that occupy your time? How many jobs do you have? Take a moment to list all of your jobs, paid and unpaid, at work and at home. Examples for a financial advisor who is also a parent might include—wealth manager, conflict resolution specialist, babysitter, cook, dog-walker, maid service, farmer, taxi driver, and personal shopper. Take a moment to list all of your jobs, paid and unpaid.

Now that you've completed your list, put a happy face next to the jobs you actually enjoy. If you put "chef" on your list because you dance around the kitchen as you prepare meals like Julia Child, then that item definitely deserves a happy face. Conversely, if you have items on the list that you enjoy as much as setting your hair on fire, draw a sad face next to them. Now, if you put a sad face next to parenting, I can't help you with that. However, you might be surprised to find that nearly everything else can be made better. **While you read this book, I want you to be on the lookout for apps that will help you get rid of your sad faces.**

Which of the following areas of your life would you like technology to help you with? Check all that apply:

- ☐ Connect with friends and family

- ☐ Find a job

- ☐ Build better business connections

- ☐ Get clients

- ☐ Improve/organize home life

- ☐ Plan and enjoy free time

See where you stack up against the 700+ busy professionals who took my technology survey:

- Connect with friends and family—48%

- Find a job—18%

- Build better business connections—76%

- Get clients—61%

- Improve/organize home life—51%

- Plan and enjoy free time—56%

Choose the tools that will help **you best accomplish your goals**, based on your answers above. If you're focusing on "building better business connections" and "organizing your home life," feel free to skip suggestions for "getting a job" in Section 4. If you're concerned that you'll become too attached to your mobile device, read "Self-Care in the Technology Age" in Section 4.

The trick is to form new daily habits around technology. Remember, a journey of a thousand miles begins with a single download or something like that. Just incorporate one little thing a day, every couple days or weekly—it's up to you! Get into the habit of creating a daily to-do list using Evernote or Todoist (we'll talk about both later), and then review that list to see what items can be outsourced or made more efficient now and in the future. Get comfortable asking yourself throughout the day, "How can I do this more efficiently?" Think about the technology at your fingertips as a possible solution.

Use your mental filter to only use the tools that will work for you right now. As for the others, leave them for another day.

You do have to make time—not a great deal of time—but set aside at least ten minutes today. Make time to learn how to save time.

One Tech
Action

Section 2: **All About Apps**

Appsolutely Fabulous!

Was the headline a bit too much? Yes? Well, excuse my enthusiasm because apps have changed my life!

For the purposes of this book, an app (short for application) is an easy-to-use downloadable program for mobile devices. Mobile devices include mobile phones, tablets, etc. On your mobile devices, apps appear as little icons. A quick peek at the iOS App Store reveals over 2 million apps available for download. And in the Google Play Store, there are over 2.2 million apps. Some apps are free and others are available at a small fee. Innumerable useful apps have a free and paid version, with the paid version offering more options or greater functionality. The vast majority of apps, I'd guess at least 80%, are for gaming and entertainment. However, even with less than 20% dedicated to business or efficiency, it's impossible for you to incorporate all advantageous apps into your daily regimen. Don't even try!

Efficiency apps are a great deal like fruits and vegetables in a supermarket. When you visit the grocery store to find healthy choices for meals, you will find innumerable types of vegetation of all different sizes, shapes, and flavors that would be great for providing nutrients for your body. However, you only have a certain amount of room in your stomach per meal, so you don't purchase the entire produce section. You buy what you can reasonably consume. Download only the number of efficiency apps that you can adequately utilize.

You may notice that some of your favorite apps are missing in this book. In the interest of keeping this resource as concise as possible, we are focusing on the top apps that will serve the largest number of busy professionals.

For every app, there are at least two other apps that serve the exact same purpose or function. If you are currently using one of the alternative apps, and it's working for you, that's fine. Do not get rid of what's already working for you to replace it with my recommendation unless my suggested app offers features, lacking in the app you're already using, that would benefit you. Occasionally, I will mention two competitor apps. The reasoning behind this is there are a large number of users leveraging each application and either option is equally helpful. In some cases, some apps service areas that others do not. Choose the one that will work best for you. All of the apps discussed in this section are simply suggestions, so only use those that will support you in accomplishing your specific goals. Use this chapter as a reference source where you can look back and learn about different apps. If an app is "cool" but is not going to help you with your goals, please do not download it to your mobile device.

In order to effectively use apps, you must have space on your mobile device. If you are currently lacking space, consider buying a new device (especially if your current device is more than a couple years old). If possible, free up memory by deleting unnecessary apps and by moving videos and photos from your mobile device to your computer or the cloud.

Not all the service-based apps mentioned in this section will be available where you live. Many of them roll out in the largest markets and then move on to other locations. If an app that I mentioned is not available to you at the moment, consider searching Google to see if a competitor's app is offered near you. In many cities, smaller businesses have been established to fill the void left by larger apps that have not begun to operate in that vicinity.

Some of us become stagnant because we're always searching for "the very best." Imagine you have an intense hunger and are moments from losing consciousness. Do you bite into the crunchy, albeit slightly bruised, Washington apple in your palm, or do you delay eating and walk to the grocery store a mile away to get a fresh, organic Honeycrisp? It's a better choice to use an app that's good enough to help you accomplish your goals now, rather than to keep searching around for the one that could be superior, and still be searching and in limbo two years later. Take immediate action with the resources you currently have at your disposal.

While I am truly a technology advocate, there are times when incorporating new apps can be a bad idea. Friends and family can lead us in the wrong direction. On one occasion, my sister suggested that I download an app she had been using for video chat, so I could chat with her and my baby nephew. It was supposedly an alternative to Face-Time, which allows you to video chat. Within seven minutes of downloading the app to my phone, the following is what I was faced with:

I didn't know my fingers could move so fast—I couldn't get that app off my phone fast enough! As an aside, there really are some remarkably weird people online. Like, really, really weird. The point is we all have hiccups, even technology strategists.

You have a wide selection of helpful apps to choose from—with some even able to inject a little humor into your life. How many times have you ever frequented a movie theater and needed to use the restroom, but were afraid you would miss an essential part of the movie's plot? The RunPee app alerts you to when it's safe to take a bathroom break during a film, so you won't miss an important scene. It sounds funny, but it's amazingly practical. On the other hand, some apps border on bizarre, if not dangerous. The Spoonr app enables you to quickly locate people near you, through GPS, who are game for an immediate cuddle session. Even more, you can see how they've been ranked in the past by other cuddlers. While I carry no judgment regarding people using apps to physically meet up, my spidey sense tells me that you might end up in some unfortunate or at least uncomfortable situations using this app. My advice: not safe, my friend.

You'll also encounter social media apps in this chapter. In this book, I'm focusing on specific action items aimed at using these social media apps for efficiency versus making you a social media expert or creating a social media marketing strategy. If you would like to learn more about social media and how to use it as a professional, check out my other book, *The Social Media Why: A Busy Professional's Practical Guide to Using Social Media Including LinkedIn, Facebook, Twitter, YouTube, Pinterest, Google+ and Blogs for Business.*

Do I Have Enough Space for Apps?

In this app-intensive environment with users storing entire music collections, videos, and hundreds of photos on their phones, ideally, one should have a minimum of 32GB of total storage space. For types who are extra-techie-techie-pants, 64GB of storage is perfect. As for me? I have a 128GB Samsung and 128GB iPhone. Please don't judge me—I buy this stuff, so I can teach you about it!

If you're using an Android, open the Settings screen and tap Storage. It'll show you how much space you have available.

On an iOS device, launch the Settings app, choose the General tab, and then the About tab. Scroll until you see the Available option.

Where to Get Apps

In comparing worldwide market shares, Android accounts for 80.7% of sales, iOS for 17.7%, Windows for 1.1%, and Blackberry for 0.2%. In my own survey, 66.4% of respondents use iOS, 32.2% use an Android, 1% use Windows, and 0.3% use a Blackberry. I'm sharing this data as a fancy way of saying that I'm only focusing on iOS and Android mobile-device apps in this book because that's what nearly 99% of you are using.

Also, it bears mentioning that iOS is an operating system used for mobile devices manufactured by Apple Inc., while Android is a mobile-operating system developed by Google.

Finding Apps on iOS

If you're operating an iOS (Apple) device, you'll find your apps in the App Store, which at the time of this publication has the following icon.

After clicking on the App Store icon, you'll be taken into the store. To find a specific app, click on the search box with the magnifying glass, and type in the name of the app. Once you become more advanced, having already instituted your chosen action items from this book, you may want to click on the Explore button on the home screen to view categories such as Business, Education, Finance, Health & Fitness, and more!

When considering which app might be best for a particular need, click on the app name and the review tab to see its rating and how many people rated it. Unlike Android, Apple does not provide download statistics. Select the Related tab to see which apps are competitors or complement your selection. While selecting the best apps for your needs, consider features along with its ratings and the number of raters. Obviously, newly released apps will not have as many ratings as older competitors.

Finding Apps on Android

If you have an Android (Google product) device, you'll download your apps from the Play Store, which at the time of this publication has the following icon.

Once you click on the Play Store icon, you'll be taken directly into Google Play. Search for apps by typing their name directly into the Google Play search box at the top of the screen. Once you become more advanced, having already instituted your chosen action items from this book, you may want to click on the Categories tab on the home screen to view categories such as Business, Communication, Education, Finance, and more!

When considering which app might be best for a particular need, click on the app name and review the number of downloads, the ratings (look at how many people rated it), and the Similar tab to see which apps are competitors. Typically, the best apps are those with the highest ratings and most users. An exception would be if the app was recently released, which would mean that it hasn't had the time to garner the number of users as its older predecessors.

Stay Safe

What the Experts Say

Cybersecurity is a valid concern for anyone using computers or mobile devices. For this reason, I interviewed two experts in the space, James Morrison and Robert Siciliano.

James Morrison is a Computer Scientist with the Federal Bureau of Investigation assigned to the Houston Division. He serves as a local technical expert to the Special Agents and Task Force Officers on the Houston Area Cyber Crimes Task Force. He has worked in the IT field for more than 27 years, including 18 years with the FBI.

Robert Siciliano, CSP, the #1 bestselling Amazon.com author and CEO of IDTheftSecurity.com, may get your attention with his engaging tone and approachable personality—but he is serious about teaching fraud prevention and personal security. He is a personal security and identity theft expert and speaker. Siciliano is also the author of *99 Things You Wish You Knew Before Your Identity Was Stolen*.

Under each question, you'll notice the experts' responses as well as my own non-techie translation.

Which product is typically safer? Android or Apple?

Robert: Without a doubt iOS devices are much more secure. There are few if any known exploits in regards to iPhones or iPads. There are tens of thousands of them that are targeting the Android devices; these are known viruses that will function similarly to how viruses function on a Windows PC.

Google's operating system, Android, is what is considered an open source system, meaning the code is readily available. Anybody can access the code, and they can build software around it. That includes building a virus around that code. Whereas iOS, Apple's operating system, is not open source. There's only a certain allotted amount of code available for developers to build their software around, and that keeps Apple that much more secure, due to the nature of that software.

James: Malware developers can subvert a legitimate program or get their malware submitted into the appropriate mobile stores. This is where the Apple's security model seems more robust. Even if you get the malicious application past the vetting process, Apple appears to be quick to remove an app once it has been determined to be malicious. The various Android stores each show different response times to a reported malicious app, and their vetting processes are also different across the various stores, with the Android security model relying more on the user to determine whether an application is "good" or "bad."

Crystal's Non-Techie Translation: Apple's iOS devices are generally safer than Android devices. Android gives the world its "blueprint" for free because several brands make Android phones, unlike iOS devices that are solely made by Apple. If everyone (that includes home builders, neighbors, and robbers) had access to your home's blueprint, it would make it easier for thieves to sneak into your home and navigate around. It's, also, more difficult to place a malicious app into Apple's App Store than Google's Play Store.

How can smart phone users protect themselves?

James: The best security for physical loss or theft is encrypting the data. This is done automatically on Apple phones if the PIN/Password is set. Android makes encryption optional. If you feel your phone is a target, encrypting the data at least protects the data. Also make sure the PIN/Password is legitimately complex. Putting 123456 for a PIN or password is almost useless. Weak or compromised passwords are still one of the largest sources of data breaches. If each of us would just change our passwords on a regular basis and use different passwords across different sites, it would make our devices a lot safer.

When dealing with malicious mail/SMS messages, the best way to protect from this remains to be vigilant. If you get an SMS message from an unknown number, delete it. There is absolutely no reason to click on the link, and yet people still do this every day. What is interesting is that most people will not answer a phone call from a strange number, but a strange text message is not viewed as malicious, and it can be. Malicious messages can come to your phone as well. Clicking on a link in a message from an unknown sender runs the risk of infecting your phone with malware.

In terms of unwanted access, connecting your phone to other networks can be dangerous. One attack we have seen is called Juice Jacking, and it involves someone using a charging kiosk and the kiosk having its connections compromised so that instead of plugging in for just a charge, you are actually plugging your phone into a device which can then access your data. If a window pops up asking to grant access, the answer is no. A large part of security is being watchful—if you see a window popping up that doesn't look right, it probably isn't.

Robert: Consumers have to be cyber scam aware, as there are a number of scams that can occur. One involves SMS, which are text messages.

When you click links, they can affect your device. Sometimes when you click those links, it might bring you to a spoofed website that is basically a fake website designed to extract your credentials, including passwords and credit card information. Beyond being cyber scam aware, anti-virus protection is a necessity for Android phones. When you have an Android, you need to actually install anti-virus protection the same way you install it on a Windows machine.

Crystal's Non-Techie Translation: Choose a strong password for your phone. If you have an Android device, install anti-virus software. Be aware of possible scams. Do not ever click on links in text messages sent from numbers you don't know! Be careful where you charge your phone! If, while charging at a kiosk, you get a pop-up window asking you for access to any part of your phone, just say no! Before entering passwords or credit card information, ensure that you're on a "real" site. For instance, there is a big different between being on Paypal.com and Paypalforpayments.com.

How do you determine if an app is safe?

James: I tend to not install apps until they have been around a little while. Read the reviews and ask others if they use the app. Do a little research. Most people will not do research because they install applications on a whim. They may be bored with their current suite of games or apps, and they will look through the store for something new. Or, they see a link on another application (i.e., social media) and follow that link to a store. When you decide to install an app, watch the permissions asked for by the application. Yes, you may have to read them. If you don't like what is being asked for, don't allow the install. Even after installing, watch for strange behavior on your device. When you decide you do not want the application anymore, uninstall it. Many mobile devices have tons of unwanted applications that were installed and are no longer used, but have not been cleaned out.

Robert: The rule of thumb (as they say) is to make sure you're downloading from approved stores. Apple's App Store and Google Play are approved. Once you start going beyond those two, then you can get yourself into trouble. Third-party resources/stores/applications, which are not vetted or approved by the App Store and Google Play, are where people can get in trouble.

With iPhones, and apps specific to iPhones, you're not going to be able to download an app to an iPhone unless you jail break your iPhone. Jail breaking is a process where you install software on an iPhone that breaks down the operating system in a way that allows the iPhone to function beyond the walls guarded by the iOS App Store. When you download apps on a jailbroken iPhone, you are at risk of installing apps that will make a mess of your device, spy on you, and create malware.

Crystal's Non-Techie Translation: Only download apps from Google Play or Apple's App Store. Make sure the apps have been around for a while and have a few hundred (at least) ratings. Apps require permissions. **Read what it's asking to access before you download it.** If you don't feel comfortable with the permissions requested, don't download it. Be logical. Your bank app requests access to your camera not because WellsFargo is spying on you, but because it needs your camera to deposit checks.

What should people keep in mind before they download browser extensions?

Robert: You should without a doubt have an updated version of whatever browser you have—Chrome, Firefox, Opera, or Internet Explorer. Having the latest updated version of your operating system is equally as essential. When it comes to protecting your devices, whether they are tablets, mobiles, PCs, Macs, etc., critical security revolves around updated operating systems, critical security patches, updated browsers, updated software in general, and that means no matter what software you are using: Adobe Flash, Microsoft office, you name it. Make sure you have anti-virus, anti-spyware, anti-phishing and a firewall—all are fundamentals of digital security.

James: I think the main risk associated with browser extensions is knowing what the additional functionality gives up on the security side. To use some extensions, the user may have to activate another web technology that may have vulnerabilities. For example, if the extension is written in JavaScript, and you have to enable this to get the extensions to work, are the vulnerabilities of JavaScript worth the additional functionality? As with any "after-market" modifications to the base product, you may have unintended behaviors and those have to be weighed as well.

Crystal's Non-Techie Translation: Make sure you have good anti-virus software on your computer and ensure that you're running the most updated version of your browser—whether Safari, Firefox, Chrome, Internet Explorer, etc. Understand that you're giving up some security for the benefits of using extensions. It may be beneficial, prior to down-loading, to perform a simple Google search for the desired extension's name plus the word "security" to see what pops up.

Five Tips for Staying Safe

Not all apps available for download are safe, but the tools mentioned in this book are well known and widely used. Outside of actual privacy concerns that you may have (levels of desired privacy vary among technology users), they are considered to be fairly safe. It's important to bear in mind that an extension can be created by an ethical individual, and then sold to someone else later who abuses the permissions you've granted it. Also, while iOS devices are considered by most experts to be more secure than Android devices and are statistically less likely to be targeted by cybercriminals, everyone should still be vigilant.

1. Before downloading an app or browser extension, read reviews and find out more about the developer (person[s] who created it). If there isn't enough information on the developer, or if the app has relatively few ratings, pass on it.

2. Read full permissions before downloading apps and extensions. Understand what you're giving it access to, and use common sense. If you're downloading an app that works based on voice command, it stands to reason you'll have to give it access to your device's microphone.

3. Official browser extensions made by companies associated with a service typically carry less risk. For example, it's better to download a Google extension than an extension from a brand you never heard of, or, if you're using ToDoIst and want it to function from your browser, it is better to download the official version from ToDoIst versus a third-party one that was created to work with it.

4. Some browser extensions include spyware which track your online behaviors, and then sell that information to third parties or simply produce ads based on what they find. I did not find the extensions presented in this book on any lists for this behavior.

5. If you would like an extra layer of security on your phone or computer, especially if you have an Android device, consider downloading a security app or program from a large, recognized brand such as McAfee, Norton, Avast!, or TrendMicro.

Meet the Apps

In this chapter, you'll find top apps for efficiency. There is a key provided below. Next to the app name, you'll find the icons $\bigcirc$, $\triangle$ or $ indicating fees associated with the app. Next to that, you'll see an icon representing the area(s) of efficiency that the app will help with. Feel free to read all the way through or, if you want to get started quickly, only look at the apps that will help you achieve your goals. For instance, if you're only interested in finding employment, feel free to only look at the apps with the corresponding icon. Also, the icons are based on how the average person would most likely use the app. If you happen to think of a creative way to use an app for efficiency not suggested in this book, go for it!

You may notice that some of your favorite apps are missing. That's not an oversight. In the interest of brevity and in only presenting the apps most likely to be helpful to the largest number of busy people, not all great apps are included in this book.

Price Key

○ = Free

△ = Fee or Upgrade Available

$ = Paid Service Only

Area of Efficiency Key

= Connect with Friends and Family

= Find a Job

= Build Better Business Connections

= Get Clients

= Improve/Organize Home Life

= Personal Development

= Plan and Enjoy Free Time

 **Airbnb**

Airbnb, a member of the sharing economy, is an online marketplace that enables everyday people to list, find, and rent vacation homes. You may use Airbnb if you want to travel somewhere and experience "local" life, if you want to save money (as sometimes it is less expensive than hotels, especially, if you plan to cook your own food), or if hotels in a particular destination are sold out. At the same time, you can also rent your own home (pending local laws and community rules). Rent an entire home or a room. The app is very easy to use, featuring filters that allow you to search by preferences and the ability to see ratings and comments from past guests. The app is totally free. You pay for the accommodations. HomeAway and VRBO (Vacation Rentals by Owner—actually owned by HomeAway) are Airbnb's direct competitors.

 Airline Apps ○

If you fly frequently, you may want to consider downloading your preferred airline's app. The apps typically allow you to make reservations, change reservations, generate an e-ticket, and access in-flight entertainment.

Amazon

The world's largest online retailer is also one of the greatest efficiency tools! Get nearly anything you can think of delivered via this app. Do you need lawn chairs for a get-together next weekend, but your schedule is packed? Amazon. Need to purchase Christmas gifts but don't want to engage in WWE-style extreme shopping at your local stores? Amazon. Plus, with Prime membership, currently $99 per year, two-day delivery is free. As an aside, you will also have the ability to borrow books from the Kindle Owners' Lending Library at no cost. Amazon has also rolled out a service called Amazon Prime Now where Prime customers in select metro areas can receive same-day delivery of items ranging from groceries to electronics. Last minute babysitting duty? Order toys and books and have them at your doorstep before the kids arrive! The app is free; you pay for purchases.

Audible

Audible is the preeminent audiobook app. Owned by Amazon, it allows you to listen to your favorite books anywhere, with more than 180,000 titles available for download to your device. One of my favorite features of Audible is its ability to mark exactly where you left off on a recording. So, whether I listen to the book from my iPhone or I pick it up later from my Android device, it knows the last place I left off, and asks if I'd like to start where I left off on the other device. With Audible, you can purchase a monthly membership which allows you a certain amount of credits per month or you can purchase books as you want them. Tip: Only use book credits toward books that cost more than the monthly membership fee. For instance, don't use a book credit that you're paying $14.95 for to buy and download a book that costs $9.99. Pay for that one and save your credit for the other book you want for $23.95.

 ### Banking Apps

Banking apps are applications provided by banks for their banking customers. Many banks, such as Chase, Bank of America, and Wells Fargo, offer clients the ability to perform actions like transfer funds between their accounts, instantly send money to others, check bank balances, and even deposit checks using the app. While rules vary from bank to bank, most of the larger banks limit you to depositing checks with an amount of no more than $1,000.

Blue Apron

A subscription meal-delivery service, Blue Apron provides all the ingredients and instructions needed to prepare meals for as little as two people or as many as six. It features the ability to select dietary preferences (great news for vegetarians, like me—yay!), and the ingredients arrive to your door with ice packs. The pricing per person is more than you'd spend if you made an at-home meal or casserole, but less than most of us would spend eating out at an inexpensive sit-in restaurant. Top competitors include Plated and HelloFresh. Green Chef is a wonderful alternative for people who need vegetarian, vegan, gluten-free and even paleo options. At the time of publication, the app is only available for iOS devices, although anyone can sign up for the service and manage their accounts via their website.

 Evernote

Evernote is, in my opinion, one of the best organization platforms in existence. It empowers you to easily store and organize information (ideas, projects, reference material) that then syncs between all of your computers and mobile devices. Evernote enables users to store pictures, text, handwritten notes, PDFs, web pages, screen shots, scanned items, attachments (including video and audio), and so much more!

Generate notes—which can be any of the items listed above—and then store those notes in notebooks for organization. Both notes and notebooks can be shared for collaboration!

Evernote is such an effective tool that a full one quarter of this book was written via voice-to-text as I was driving using it. How do you like that for efficiency?

Let's put this into perspective. Imagine you are redecorating your home. You can easily create a folder in Evernote titled "Home Redecorating Project." Within that folder, you can save notes that are thoughts that come to you as you're driving—by adding the actual audio or by using voice-to-text. You can take pictures of items in home goods stores, save PDFs from potential contractors, save web pages from popular home decorating blogs, and share the entire folder with your spouse or interior designer, who can also add items, comments, etc.

Evernote, if used properly, can simplify your life by allowing you to free up mental space (converting all your competing thoughts into notes), and you can search those notes at a later date to find exactly what you need. You can even create checklists that you can mark off as you go!

For more information on Evernote plans, visit https://evernote.com/pricing/.

 Facebook

With over one billion users, Facebook is the largest social network in the world. Facebook is a powerful relationship-building engine, perfect for attracting business referrals.

The one quality that makes this network the most valuable one for building relationships is the very characteristic that sometimes gives it a bad rap—it is the most social of the social networks. Unfortunately, sometimes users get too "social" and share inappropriate items.

To be successful on Facebook, you have to make your posts about your contacts and others. There is nothing wrong with talking about yourself, but be sure to use "we" more than "I." The best networkers are people who care about others and make them feel special. Well, if Facebook is the most social and social networks are about building relationships, then, of course, you need to highlight others and make them feel good!

Unlike LinkedIn that only allows a single profile picture or Twitter, which only allows updates of 140 characters or less, Facebook allows you to post entire picture albums, notes, and much more! Of course, this also means there are many more ways you can get yourself into trouble if you are not careful about what you share and post.

Using the Facebook app, you can interact with connections, create invites and rsvp for events, engage in groups, comment on pages, and more! Unfortunately, if you want to engage in one-on-one conversations, you must have a completely separate app—Messenger—installed on your mobile device.

 FaceTime

FaceTime is a free app that allows iOS users to make one-on-one video or voice calls. All iOS users wanting to use the app must have forward-facing cameras.

 **Fancy Hands**

Fancy Hands is a service that allows you to finally have your own personal assistant! Hire U.S.-based assistants to perform tasks. Make both standard (answered within 24 hours) and live (connects you with an assistant within one minute) requests. Have you ever needed to make a doctor's appointment, but didn't have the time? Have you needed to talk to your cable service provider, but didn't have the time to hold forever to get through to the right person? Fancy Hands can make that appointment and call that provider and conference you in when a real person is on the phone. They can schedule home services, buy tickets, do online research, and much more!

 **Fiverr**

Fiverr is a global online marketplace offering tasks and services, beginning at a cost of five dollars per job completed. Be careful visiting the site; it's easy to become sucked in when you consider all of the services you can purchase for just five dollars! You can have a puppeteer create a happy birthday video for your child, have someone mail your enemy glitter or even have a contractor create a flyer for your neighborhood barbeque. All jobs start at five dollars with upgraded options available. Check your contractor's ratings from other customers. The app is free—pay per project.

 Google Docs

If you're looking for an easy-to-use resource for creating documents that can also be edited and marked up online with a group, Google Docs is the best free resource. It is an online word processor that facilitates collaboration in creating and formatting text documents in real time. The Google Docs format is extremely similar to Microsoft Word. Like Word, it offers templates for a variety of document types (e.g., letters and flyers) and the ability to track changes by user. It also offers in-document research, voice typing, and document translation. As an aside, if you have a need, you may want to check out Google Sheets (online spread sheets not unlike Excel), Google Slides (online slide maker similar to PowerPoint), and Google Forms (online survey and form creator). All of these options are free sister-companions to Google Docs.

Google Drive

Google Drive is a place for you to store files, making them accessible from any smartphone, tablet, or computer. Files including documents, videos, photos, and more are backed up safely so you can't lose them. Once stored, you can easily invite others to view them or to leave comments on any of your files or folders. Google Drive is not a replacement for Evernote or OneNote. While they all allow for file storage, I find that Google Drive is better for collaboration. It allows users to make comments on files, track edits, and research particular words straight from Google Drive, and it's easier to navigate for shared purposes. When I want someone to have access to a folder to read or to simply add more files, I use Evernote or OneNote. When I want to collaboratively create documents or other projects, I use Google Drive. Google Docs, Sheets, Slides, and Forms are all stored in Google Drive.

 Google Maps

Google Maps is a web-mapping service that features street maps, satellite imagery, street views in 360°, real-time traffic conditions, and route planning for traveling by car, walking, bicycling or using public transportation. If you have an iOS device, you might say, "I already have Maps on my device." Yes, you do. Now, download Google Maps and use it instead. While iOS Maps is certainly good, Google Maps is often more accurate with directions, and I've found it to be much more accurate with road conditions and times.

 Google Translate

Translate between languages by typing in phrases or speaking directly into your phone using Google Translate. The app also offers instant camera translation and the ability to draw characters instead of using the keyboard. Use this app to communicate with locals when you travel, to communicate with a friends visiting from another country, or to help you figure out what a phrase means in a bilingual movie!

 *Groupon*

Groupon delivers deals between 50% and 70% off activities and products in more than 500 cities across the globe. The app allows you to buy and redeem deals and track your purchases and expiration dates.

If you're looking for fun wallet-friendly family activities, Groupon is an efficient way to find something fast. I've used it to purchase painting classes with friends, horseback riding lessons for my husband and me, and tickets to numerous museums for my nephew.

 ## *Hangouts*

Hangouts is a robust Google app that allows you to take advantage of free messaging, video, and voice. Use Hangouts to message friends, start a free video or voice call, or even have a conversation with a group. This app is available across platforms. You can have a video chat with up to ten people or a group voice chats for up to 150 people! Call any number around the world, and, if the user is also a Hangout user, the call will be free! You can also use Hangouts for SMS/MMS text (regular texting) and messaging. Although the platform is from Google, it is available on both Android and iOS devices.

 ## *Hospital Apps*

Some hospital organizations, such as Kelsey-Seybold, have apps where their customers can access their patient information, refill prescriptions, and make appointments.

 **Instacart**

Instacart is a grocery shopping service, not unlike Postmates (mentioned later). It is a part of the sharing economy where everyday people shop and deliver groceries. While you can use Postmates for grocery delivery, which I have done, it's considerably more efficient to use Instacart. The app features grocery store partners in your area. For each store, they preload a list of inventory to choose from, in addition to allowing you the option of placing custom requests. Instead of listing grocery items and having to think of the exact item names and brands as you would with Postmates, with Instacart, you can simply click on pictures and descriptions that are already preloaded. Search by name or category. The app is free; you pay for groceries and service.

 LinkedIn

LinkedIn is a powerful social network that helps you exchange knowledge, resources, and career and business opportunities with over 430 million professionals. LinkedIn is a cross between a resume bank, a yellow pages directory, and a business chat forum. LinkedIn gives you the ability to build and control your personal online brand, increasing the chances of influential decision-makers finding you on the web.

LinkedIn is truly the no-nonsense social network. It caters to a sophisticated audience of career professionals. In fact, every Fortune 500 company is represented on the site. Another great thing about LinkedIn—it is the simplest to maintain. You don't have to worry about others posting things on your profile or needing to post numerous times throughout the day.

LinkedIn is the only social network where it is acceptable to make your profile 100 percent about you and your accomplishments. Think of it as a super-duper resume. You want to put your best foot forward to build credibility, to get others to weigh in on how awesome you are, and to attract opportunities.

LinkedIn's user base includes CEOs, hiring managers, potential clients, friends, and any other type of professional you can think of. However, remember you don't know most of these people. LinkedIn is not a place to immediately go to and strike deals, selling people on you or your business. It is not like shooting fish in a barrel. People will report you and your account will be terminated. When you first meet someone, in-person or online, you must build trust with them as they owe you zero favors. In other words, don't ask new contacts for anything, including a sale. Instead, just as in real life, focus on building relationships. If you build rapport by demonstrating your expertise, being helpful (giving first), and being consistent, those zeros will change over time.

While the LinkedIn app is free, the network offers a variety of plans that allow users to leverage different functions. The free plan is more than sufficient for most users. With the free plan, you can still send direct messages via the app (hear that Facebook?), create posts, moderate groups, and more.

 **Messenger** *(Facebook)*

Do you want to send direct (private) messages or engage in a group message on Facebook from your mobile device? You'll need to download a completely separate app for that. According to Facebook's Mark Zuckerberg, they created a separate app for sending messages because using the original Facebook app for messaging was inefficient. In an effort to cut down on steps (click on the Facebook app, then click on the Messenger icon versus just opening the Messenger app) and make messaging faster on the platform, the distinct Messenger app was created.

 **Nextdoor**

Nextdoor is a private social network just for you and your neighbors. After confirming a user's physical address through one of three methods, users can then interact with neighbors: giving items away, issuing warnings, or asking for references for local products or services. How often have you had a nice item that you didn't want to sell, but simply wanted to go to a good home? This app is more efficient and safer than Craigslist because all users have to give their physical address and confirm it. Plus, you get to build goodwill with your neighbors! If your neighborhood is not already listed, although most are, you can start it up yourself!

 OneNote

Owned by Microsoft and very slightly more user-friendly than Evernote, OneNote allows users to organize notes from meetings, ideas, and collaborative projects all in one place. Like Evernote, OneNote allows you to sync notes between devices. If Evernote functions like a digital file cabinet, OneNote operates more like a digital notebook in terms of its look.

OneNote allows users to store a variety of items including notes, web pages, and files. It also leverages OCR, so that text in pictures is also searchable in your notebooks.

OneNote excels when it comes to handwriting notes using a stylus or your finger on your device. It allows additional features for handwritten notes that Evernote does not. The app itself is free, but with an Office 365 subscription you get access to more features.

 OpenTable

Make online reservations instantly, see restaurant reviews from diners, and earn points toward free meals. Like TripAdvisor, you can easily find restaurants near you and review feedback. However, the primary benefit this app offers is the ability to see open reservation slots for restaurants! You can quickly make a reservation and manage that reservation from within the app!

Out of Milk

Sync grocery lists across devices with Out of Milk. With this app, you'll always have your shopping list handy. The pantry list keeps track of your cupboard items such as spices and other essentials, so you always know what you have at home. The app allows you to create multiple shopping lists and sync your lists with others in real time. Now your family members can also add things to the list as needed. You can also share lists by text or email. It also displays a grand total and a running total on your shopping list. Lastly, you can browse and search local grocery deals and promotions.

 OverDrive

OverDrive is similar to Audible, but it's free! Borrow e-books, audio-books, and streaming video from your local library with this app. Like Audible, you can listen to your favorite books, but this doesn't require any type of monthly fees or purchases. Most U.S. libraries use Over-Drive to distribute their audiobook collection. You can even place holds on books; your selection will be automatically checked out to you once it becomes available. So, if you've been meaning to catch up on the newest best seller or if you'd like to learn a new language, OverDrive might be a great option for you to do so at no cost. Some libraries also use Hoopla (an OverDrive competitor) with or in place of OverDrive.

 Pharmacy Apps

Pharmacy apps, such as those provided by Walgreens, CVS, and Rite Aid, can keep their customers in the loop in regards to their account. Customers can refill prescriptions, track prescriptions, receive Rx reminders, print photos, and create photo gifts from their phones or social media. Additionally, they can receive in-store coupons and access pre-store sales, check services and insurance, and more. Some of them even allow you to skip the in-person doctor's appointment, and let you schedule video chats with real doctors, or hold a place in line at local clinics!

 Postmates

Postmates is a personal delivery service, picking up items from restaurants or storefronts that don't offer delivery service. Like Uber,

Postmates allows everyday people to utilize their own vehicles. Post-mates delivers from places like The Cheesecake Factory, fast-food restaurants, clothing stores, or office supply brands. While you may think it's just easier to drive to the stores that you need to purchase items from, there are times when it's more efficient to utilize a service like Postmates. For instance, you can use Postmates to get food delivered to your office when a client meeting runs over or to place an order to have a presentation remote (slide advancer) picked up for your 10 a.m. meeting from the comfort of your hotel room. Regrettably, Postmates is not available in all areas at the time of this publication. However, it does have several competitors, including Favor and GrubHub. If Postmates is not yet available in your area, be sure to check DoorDash (a major competitor that covers larger areas), and do a Google search to see if a local company has created a local alternative. The app is free; you pay for items ordered and service.

 ## *Scannable*

Scannable is a scanning app that works along with Evernote. Use it to scan documents using your phone's camera. After you scan, it then converts the picture into a scanned document. It even works for multiple pages! I find that I can scan a 20-page document on a seat in an airport in less than two minutes. When scanned, you have the option to simply save in Evernote or even share or send in an email. Currently available only in iOS, but their support states that they are working on an Android version.

 ## Square Register

Square register is a free app that equips you with everything you need to take payments, accepting both debit cards and credit cards with the Square magnetic strip reader. Funds are deposited fast—as soon as one to two business days. The app is free and the magstripe reader itself comes at no cost. Do you have a friend or family member who has owed you $200 for the last year and always claims that they don't have any cash on them? Well, next time they attempt to use the excuse of not having cash, pull out your handy Square reader that's hardly much larger than a quarter and ask them for a credit card! Square takes a percentage of the charge as a fee. To view Square's current fee structure, visit https://squareup.com/help/us/en/article/5068-what-are-square-s-fees.

 **TaskRabbit**

Do you need help doing something on the fly? TaskRabbit connects you with same-day help. Using the app, select from a list of popular chores. You can choose a same-day appointment or a future time that suits your schedule. Manage your booking directly in the app. You're able to chat with the Tasker and pay electronically when the task is completed. Taskers undergo an extensive background check and in-person onboarding before joining the TaskRabbit community. While you can use the service for things, such as furniture assembly and running errands, don't hesitate to use a little imagination. Want to get your spouse the newest piece of technology or tickets to an event without standing in a ridiculously long line? Hire a Tasker to stand in line, and you can swoop in at the last minute to make the purchase! Use a Tasker to help you purge your closet or storage area! The possibilities are endless. The app is free; you pay only for completed tasks.

 ToDoIst

ToDoIst is an application for personal and professional productivity. It allows users to manage their short- and long-term tasks from a mobile device or computer. For the more advanced user, it's a project management app allowing you to collaborate with teams (at work or at home) on shared tasks. The app is free, but it also has a paid version with additional features. ToDoIst's biggest competitors are Wunderlist and Any.Do.

 TripAdvisor

TripAdvisor allows millions of travelers to review, take photos, and share maps. With over 225 million reviews and opinions by travelers, TripAdvisor makes it easy to find the lowest airfare, best hotels, great restaurants, and fun things to do. Use the "near me now" feature to discover options near you. Download maps and see reviews in cities all over the world.

 TripIt

TripIt allows users to become their own travel agents, to plan every detail of their trip including lodging, rental car, and even restaurants. Create custom itineraries by hand or forward confirmation emails from flight, rental car, train tickets, and hotel companies to plans@tripit.com. TripIt will construct the itinerary. The paid pro version sends you real-time updates on flights, finds alternate flights, keeps track of awards points, and notifies you when you're eligible for a flight refund or cost savings. WorldMate is a notable competitor, though it is more focused on business travel.

 *Twitter*

Twitter is a powerful social network that acts as an efficiency tool to help professionals save time, identify key contacts, gain valuable information, and discover potential customers and job opportunities.

Twitter allows users to quickly and concisely express things that are important to them and to connect with other people who value the same things. Notice the word "concisely"—because you only get 140 characters. That means people have to get to the point.

You can solicit recommendations for services, check on the safety of family members during a natural disaster, follow all your news sources in one place, and even keep track of desired future employers. Ignore the way in which pop stars and athletes use Twitter, that will not work for you, nor is it an efficient use of time to constantly tweet selfies (unless you're being paid for product placement in them) or have wars of words.

Instead, consider this to be one of the richest and most easy-to-access pools of information in the world. Use the search box to follow conversations on specific topics or using hashtags—words/short codes starting with a pound or number sign that index a topic. You don't need to tweet to get the most out of Twitter!

 Uber

Uber is a rideshare app that is a part of the sharing economy. The sharing economy is everyday people finding ways to leverage their resources like their homes, cars, or time to make money. These services are interrupters to standard services. Uber is a direct competitor of taxi companies and transportation companies. Although there's still a debate about the safety of companies like Uber because their drivers are not required to have the same level of background checks as most taxi drivers, I personally feel safer in an Uber because when I use the app, because it knows who I'm getting into the car with. The app knows my name, my last location, and the identity of my driver. As a woman often traveling alone, I find comfort in that fact. Also, I like the fact that when I use my app to book an Uber, I can see the estimated time of pick up and where the Uber is located in real time. Uber's biggest competitor is Lyft.

 **Upwork**

Use Upwork to hire contractors or teams of experts to do any type of work from a computer. Hire someone for web design or graphic design. Perhaps, you need a new resume or want to develop your very own app! It's easy to think of this as a resource only for work; however, you can use this in your personal life as well. Hire a legal professional for contract-writing or a researcher to look into your family history or a translator to translate a "welcome to the family" note you wrote in your new brother-in-law's native language. Select your budget (overall or per hour) and allow contractors to bid for your business. You're able to review their statistics, including the number of hours they've worked on the platform, their ratings, past projects, and much more! The app itself is free; you will pay for individual jobs.

 YouTube

YouTube is a hugely popular social network that allows users to share, comment on, and perform minor editing of videos. Over one billion unique users visit YouTube each month, and over 72 hours of video are added every minute. YouTube has radically changed the way people search online. In fact, it is the second largest search engine. Do you want to learn how to share a note in Evernote or change the grocery store in Instacart? I assure you that there are several videos on the topic. If there is something you do not know how to do, online or in "real life," there is likely a video offering step-by-step directions. Want to know how to stop receiving emails from Twitter? Type "how to stop Twitter emails" in YouTube's search box. YouTube is a new social media user's best friend. Almost all of the content on YouTube is free.

 ### Zoom

Zoom provides video conferencing and desktop sharing via desktop or mobile device. Its plans range from free (50 participants for up to 40 minutes) to $19.99 per month per host. While this is not, in my opinion, the best video-conferencing software, it's a great free and user-friendly option for planning with a group of people. Think reunion planning! I would not suggest using Zoom for professional conferencing, although some users do. However, it's a cool tool for family, friends, and community projects.

One Tech

Action

Section 3: **Intelligent Assistants, Extensions, and More**

Intelligent Assistants

Intelligent assistants are simply software agents with the ability to perform tasks for its user. Siri, Google Now, and Cortana are all examples of intelligent assistants made by the major technology companies— Apple, Google, and Microsoft respectively.

Siri, Google Now, and Cortana are like your imaginary friends. The primary difference between these imaginary friends and the ones you had as a child is that they actually perform tasks to help you (and without people looking at you as if you are crazy). While there are innumerable things you can ask these assistants to do, common tasks include the following:

- Provide location-based reminders (e.g., pick up the laundry when I leave work)

- Search your emails and messages

- Purchase and download media

- Provide directions

- Set an alarm

- Send text messages

There is no cost associated with downloading intelligent assistants, and they can help you with all of your selected goal areas.

 ## *Siri*

Siri is Apple's built-in "intelligent assistant" that started with the iPhone 4S and newer iPads and iPods. Touch device users speak voice commands using natural language to operate the mobile device and its apps.

Of all the intelligent assistants, Siri has the most personality. In response to my question, "What is Cortana?" Siri replied, "That's an interesting question." When I asked her about the Google Now intelligent assistant, she answered with, "I don't really have anything to say about Google Now or ever." Ouch! To use Siri, hold down the home button and speak your command or question.

 ## *Google Now*

Google Now is an intelligent personal assistant developed by Google. Google Now is available for Android and iOS. While Google Now functions a great deal like a less funny Siri, it has some features that

Siri does not. For instance, Google Now doesn't attempt to just answer your requests, it tries to predict them! Using cards, it shares information like weather, share prices, and other data you've shown an interest in. It connects to other Google services on your phone to provide information as well. As an example, if I have an appointment in my Google Calendar, Google Now will automatically shoot me a reminder using Google Cards when I need to leave for that address, based on current traffic conditions in order to arrive on time. Privacy concerns are a legitimate issue. It's your decision how much you're willing to share. To ask Google Now for help, push and hold the home button, and then say, "Ok Google" and finish with your question/command.

 ## Cortana

Cortana is an intelligent personal assistant created by Microsoft for several platforms: Windows 10, Windows Phone 8.1, Android, and iOS. It's great for creating emails, reminders, notes, and for even opening apps. Slightly slower than its competitors—Google Now and Siri— Cortana is currently the only one of the three that runs well on both mobile devices and computers.

To use Cortana on a Windows 10 computer, simply say, "Hey Cortana," and finish your request. Make sure that you have already enabled this feature by clicking on Ask Me Anything > Gear Icon. Ensure that Let Cortana respond to "Hey Cortana" is on. While it's an option, I do not recommend that you use Cortana on your iPhone or Android as it does not have all of the capabilities on those devices as their native assistants.

Browser Extensions

A web browser extension is a piece of technology that allows a web browser—like Safari or Chrome—to perform additional actions. It's basically an app for your web browser. The most popular web browsers in the U.S., respectively, are Chrome, Internet Explorer, Safari, and Firefox. In this book, we'll look at extensions for your PCs, Macs, and larger mobile devices. Also, can I make a suggestion? If you're using Internet Explorer, you may want to consider downloading Chrome and making that your default browser instead. Many cool extensions do not work with IE (Internet Explorer). To download Chrome, visit this site: https://www.google.com/chrome/browser/desktop/.

Now, let's get started using browser extensions!

Price Key

◯ = Free

△ = Fee or Upgrade Available

$ = Paid Service Only

Area of Efficiency Key

= Connect with Friends and Family

= Find a Job

= Build Better Business Connections

= Get Clients

= Improve/Organize Home Life

= Personal Development

= Plan and Enjoy Free Time

 ### *Evernote Web Clipper*

Evernote Web Clipper is an extension for your web browser that enables you to capture full-page articles, selected text, images, important emails, and any web page you'd like to store. If you're using the Evernote app on your mobile device, you'll want to add this extension to your computer as well. At the time of this book's publication, this extension works with Chrome, Safari, Internet Explorer (IE) 7+, Firefox, and Opera.

 ### *Honey*

Have you ever searched for coupon codes when you're checking out in an online store? Coupon codes can provide amazing savings. Prior to this extension, I considered myself the queen of the coupon code, finding rare ones that saved me as much as 50% on larger purchases. This app now does the work for me, eliminating the 10–15 minutes I would normally spend scouring the web for codes. Honey automatically applies the best working codes that customers are already using to save money. At the time of this publication, Honey's browser plugin currently works on desktop versions of Chrome, Firefox, Safari, and Opera. Support for other browsers and a mobile app are coming soon, per the website.

 **Grammarly**

The Grammarly's browser extension helps users write mistake-free in social networks, Gmail, and anywhere else you write on the web. Hover over any word with an underscore to correct a mistake. It currently works with Chrome, Safari, and Firefox.

 OneNote Web Clipper

Capture any web page to OneNote, where you can easily edit, annotate, or share it. Clip only the article, recipe, or product information you really need. Access your clipped web pages from any device—even when you're offline. OneNote Web Clipper currently supports Chrome, Firefox, Internet Explorer, and Safari.

 SelfControl

SelfControl is a free app for Mac OS X that allows you to block access to distracting websites or anything else on the Internet that pulls at your productivity. You set a period of time that the sites will be blocked. You add sites to your blacklist, and click "Start." You will be unable to access those sites—even if you restart your computer or delete the application—until the timer runs down.

 StayFocusd

StayFocusd is a Chrome browser extension that helps you do just that—stay focused! Do you find yourself spending too much time on Facebook, YouTube, or other websites without getting any measurable positive results? Many of us have found ourselves in the position of being so used to checking certain websites that we do them out of habit. Use this extension to limit the amount of time that you can spend on any one website or app on your phone. It works both as an extension and an app. You can set a timer that will only allow you to spend ten minutes a day on Facebook. You can block some sites entirely. And the best part is, once you run out of time, you either have to uninstall the extension to spend more time on that site or wait until the next day.

Web Services

There are some items that are not technically apps or browser extensions, but, nonetheless, warrant mentioning for efficiency. The following are some of the top services that go hand-in-hand with leveraging technology for efficiency.

 Air and Water Filter
Delivery Services

One of the smartest decisions I made is to have my home air and water filters set up to be delivered on a recurring basis. There are many services to choose from. Most of the major refrigerator appliance companies offer a subscription option for their filters, via their websites. I use the Frigidaire subscription service. If the option is not available for your refrigerator model, simply google "water filter subscription" to select one of the many third-party services available. To find an air filter service, google "residential air filter subscription."

 **Doodle**

Doodle is a scheduling resource that allows users to quickly find a date and time to meet with multiple people. Suggest multiple dates and times for participants to meet, then Doodle creates a polling calendar that can be sent to participants for feedback. While upgrades are available, the free account is more than sufficient for the average user, who just wants to quickly schedule a meeting with multiple people.

 Google Alerts

Track when specific words or terms of interest are mentioned on the web. The service sends you an email notifying you of the mention based on your preference: as it happens, once a day, or once per week. Want to know when "apartment for rent in San Francisco" pops up somewhere online or when someone mentions your not very common name (good luck if your name is John Smith)? Use Google Alerts to find out. It does not track words posted on most large social networks.

IFTTT

If This Then That, also known as IFTTT, is an extremely powerful efficiency and automation program. If the other tools presented in this book are like dollar-store water guns, IFTTT is like a NERF Super Soaker. Using "recipes," IFTTT allows users to create chains of simple conditional statements, which are triggered based on changes to other web services such as Gmail or Facebook. For instance, if a new listing posts to Craigslist using your specified terms (e.g., 2BDRM San Francisco), you'll receive a text with a link. Or, if an item you're following at Best Buy changes price, you can receive a text. It also works with several brands of smart appliances and cars. At the time of publication, this service is free. However, I don't expect it to stay that way.

 SendOutCards

SendOutCards is a service that allows users to create unique, one-of-a-kind thank-you cards with or without gifts, which are then mailed by the service. Add in your own picture and text or choose from the many templates available. You can even turn your handwriting into a font. Did you and a potential client take a picture together at an industry event? Turn it into a card with a message in your own writing. Have the company mail it out with a gift card to the potential client's favorite restaurant that they mentioned while you were chatting.

 ## *Shoeboxed.com*

Shoeboxed users are able to scan and organize business cards and receipts. You can upload business card contacts into your address book from an easy-to-use spreadsheet file. Save copies of your receipts to ensure they do not fade before tax time, create reports, and much more!

Zapier is an automation service that enables users to automate actions connecting separate services by using "zaps," without any coding. It runs similarly to IFTTT, but with more enterprise options. For instance, while you can automate items like Google services and social networks as with IFTTT, you can also create zaps with Constant Contact, Salesforce, Zoom, and various customer relationship management systems. For current pricing information on upgraded plans, visit https://zapier.com/pricing/.

One Tech

Action

Section 4: **Take One Simple Tech Action**

It's time to get started! Remember to ensure that you have plenty of space on your phone! If you run into any difficulties, don't hesitate to type your how-to question into Google or YouTube or, better yet, ask your personal assistant— Siri, Cortana, or Google Now!

Get Comfortable with Your Intelligent Assistant

Do you currently use your intelligent assistant regularly? If not, here is an opportunity for you to practice using your assistant. Take five minutes to practice the following commands:

 Siri

If you have not already, you'll have to enable the Hey Siri feature. Go to Settings > General > Siri, and then toggle on "Allow 'Hey Siri.'" The next time you summon Siri by holding down on the Home button or by calling out "Hey Siri" when your iOS device is plugged in, you'll be taken to a setup screen.

To get Siri to respond, press and hold the Home button and issue her a command or question. If you're using Apple's earpods, press and hold the center button and speak. Lastly, if you have Hey Siri enabled, say "Hey Siri" when your iPhone is plugged in and charging, followed by your question/command.

- Call <insert name of person from your phone book>.

- FaceTime <insert name of person from your phone book>.

- Set timer for ten minutes.

- Send email to <insert name of person in your phonebook> about <insert subject> and say <insert message>.

- Send a text message to <insert name of person in your phonebook> that says <insert message>.

- Open calendar.

- What's the weather like today?

- What's 18% of $32.65?

- Take a picture.

- Turn on airplane mode (but don't agree to it).

- What time is it in Tokyo?

- What appointments do I have tomorrow?

- Remind me to remember my keys when I leave.

- Find pictures of rainbows.

- Where is the nearest office supply store?

- Make a reservation at <insert restaurant you want to visit> for <insert time>.

- What's the nearest museum?

- Add dentist appointment tomorrow at 2 p.m.

- Take me home.

 ### Google Now

With newer Android devices, just say "Ok Google," followed by a question or task. Or, tap and hold the Home button or the microphone button in the Google search bar, and skip the "Ok Google" portion of the conversation. If "Ok Google" doesn't appear to be working, enable it. Go to Settings > Applications> Google > Settings > Voice > "Ok Google" detection.

- Call <insert name of person in your phone book>.

- Set timer for ten minutes.

- Send email to <insert name of person in your phonebook> about <insert subject> and say <insert message>.

- Send a text message to <insert name of person in your phonebook> that says <insert message>.

- Open calendar.

- What's the weather like today?

- What's 18% of $32.65?

- Take a picture.

- Turn on airplane mode (but don't agree to it).

- What time is it in Tokyo?

- What appointments do I have tomorrow?

- Remind me to remember my keys when I leave. (This command requires GPS to be turned on.)

- Find pictures of rainbows.

- Where is the nearest office supply store?

- Add dentist appointment tomorrow at 2 p.m.

- Take me home.

◯ Cortana

To get Cortana to respond, click the Cortana button on the taskbar. Don't see Cortana? Right-click the taskbar and go to Cortana > Show Cortana icon. If you have enabled "Hey, Cortana," say "Hey, Cortana," followed by your question or command. Here's how to enable "Hey, Cortana." Click on the search box>menu icon> Notebook> Settings> click "Let Cortana respond to 'Hey, Cortana.'" to On.

- Write an email to <insert name of person in your phonebook> saying <insert message>.

- Open calendar.

- Show me top headlines.

- What's the weather like?

- How many kilometers are 18 miles?

- Take a picture.

- Turn on airplane mode (but don't agree to it).

- What time is it in Tokyo?

- What appointments do I have tomorrow?

- Find pictures of rainbows.

- Who is the CEO of Microsoft?

- Open <insert program name>.

Adjust Your Settings

The name of the game is efficiency! It's distracting to receive notifications from a million different apps all day. For this reason, you'll need to become intimately familiar with your phone settings. The easiest way to do this on your mobile device would be to simply ask your intelligent assistant to "open application settings" and turn off notifications for those interruptive apps.

Start Taking One Tech Action!

If you want to continually move forward using technology, you must commit to taking action. Remember the goal areas you designated earlier? Scroll down below to your area(s) of interest. Each goal area has an average of fifty action items to choose from with additional spaces for you to add your own. Some of these actions should be performed once while others can be repeated. Decide to take one of these actions daily, biweekly, weekly, or whenever you feel like you're falling behind. Most items will take you less than five minutes!

You may notice that on some action items, I offer the option of using one of several tools. Use the tool that you have already downloaded. For instance, if I suggest that you put your daily to-do list in apps A, B, or C, and you are already using B for your grocery list, use B for your daily to-do list as well. Minimize the amount of apps/tools for maximum efficiency and smartphone space!

Connect with Friends and Family

- If you're planning an upcoming family or friends' getaway, download the Airbnb app.

- If you have purchased airline tickets to visit loved ones, download your airline's app.

- Looking for something cool to do with your family, download the Amazon app to purchase things like flag football kits, board games, and more. If you plan on buying things throughout the year, consider Amazon Prime membership for free shipping and access to additional benefits.

- Download Groupon.

- Download the Evernote or OneNote app to your phone.

- Download the Evernote Web Clipper or OneNote Web Clipper to your browser.

- Create any of the following folders in Evernote or OneNote: Fun Family Activities, Family Vacation Ideas, Family Tree, Girls' Night Ideas, or Holiday Parties.

- Create your own family-centered folders in Evernote or OneNote.

- Share folders you created in Evernote or OneNote with other family members or friends.

- Download the Facebook app.

- Connect with family and friends on Facebook.

- Create a secret family group on Facebook and invite family members.

- Create a secret friend group on Facebook and invite friends.

- Create a Facebook group/event for activities you are planning (e.g., family reunion, class reunion, family history).

- FaceTime a loved one with an iPhone.

- Read a book to a child or have her read one to you via FaceTime.

- Download Fiverr.

- Does a loved one have a birthday coming up in the next month? Use Fiverr to have someone create a custom happy birthday video, a custom piece of simple jewelry, or anything else that can be specially made.

- Are you working on a family/friends event where you'd like to share files? Download Google Drive and Google Docs.

- Upload a master family directory to Google Drive that includes names, phone numbers, addresses, and birthdays.

- Send out the share link via email, text or family Facebook group (if you created one) and ask family members to update the family directory.

- Download Google Maps to your phone. Yes, even you iOS users. Use it for driving directions or to map out walking, biking, or public transportation options with family or friends.

- If you have a family member or friend who speaks another language, or if you are planning to go to a place where English is not the primary language, download Google Translate.

- Looking to cook more creative meals for or with your family? Download the Blue Apron app and sign up for a plan.

- Buy a Groupon to a favorite or cool restaurant you'd like to try with loved ones.

- Buy a Groupon for a fun group activity—horseback riding, mystery theater, or whatever tickles your fancy!

- Want to video chat with a single person or a group of friends? Download Hangouts.

- Have a mini family/friend reunion via Hangouts.

- If you're using Facebook and want to be able to communicate with people one-on-one, download the separate Messenger app.

- Send a chat/message to multiple people using the Messenger app. Change the group name and even give users nicknames. Use this to quickly communicate with your group of family/friends.

- Download Nextdoor, sign up, and create a profile to instantly start connecting with neighbors.

- Download TripAdvisor to find good restaurant and entertainment options.

- Download OpenTable.

- Use TripAdvisor to find a fun activity or event for you and your circle to enjoy.

- Make lunch or dinner reservations for your friends and/or family using OpenTable.

- Download Tripit if you're planning any trips with friends or family.

- Share the Tripit trip information with friends and family using the app.

- Forward all confirmation emails (from hotel, airlines, etc.) to TripAdvisor in order to create a single itinerary.

- Need taxi/car service to get to/from friends? Download Uber and set up your profile.

- Need to have a planning committee meeting with friends or family for an upcoming event (e.g., reunion, faith event)? Download Zoom.

- Use Siri/Google Now to set a reminder to check Groupon once every two weeks for fun activities.

- Set a Siri/Google Now reminder to call someone on their birthday.

- If you're using Evernote or OneNote, download the corresponding Web Clipper to your browser.

- Go to Doodle.com to schedule an extended family outing or fun time out with friends. Put in a few dates/time options (I recommend 3–4) and send out to participants.

- Sign up for SendOutCards to send custom cards to friends/family.

- Set up SendOutCards for birthdays in the future. Include gifts if you like.

- Set up Google Alerts for the names of prominent family and friends in order to know when they win awards/get promotions, etc. Call them/email them/send a card when they have a new accomplishment.

- Set up a Google Alert for items that matter to your family or group of friends (e.g., cancer trials, travel destinations) and forward information as you receive it.

- Add StayFocusd or SelfControl to your browser to help free up more time to spend with family.

- Add websites to StayFocusd or SelfControl, such as Facebook, Twitter, etc.

- _____

  _____

- _____

  _____

- _____

Find a Job

- Sign up for Shoeboxed.

- Put all loose business cards into a Shoeboxed envelope and mail them off.

- Upload Shoeboxed contacts into LinkedIn and send them a connection request.

- Download the Evernote or OneNote Web app to your phone.

- Download the Evernote or OneNote Web Clipper to your browser.

- Create a folder in Evernote or OneNote for each potential place of employment.

- As you research your potential places of employment, add interesting thoughts, web clips, news about the company (found on Twitter or other places), emails from hiring managers, pictures of brochures to their folder, etc.

- Download Grammarly to your browser for additional protection for error-free online applications.

- Add StayFocusd or SelfControl to your browser.

- Add websites to StayFocusd or SelfControl, such as Facebook, Twitter, etc.

- Create a Twitter list named "Potential Jobs."

- Add five companies to your "Potential Jobs" Twitter list.

- Go to Twitter, and, in the search box, type things like "Houston jobs" or "engineer jobs Wyoming" to find potential job posting boards. For instance, the profiles @IndianapolisJbs and @Engineer_Jobs post available positions in their Twitter feed. Add them to your "Potential Jobs" list.

- Use Siri/Google Now to set a reminder once a day to check your "Potential Jobs" Twitter list and job boards that you're following.

- Set up a Google Alert for job listings that meet your criteria (e.g., hotel director of sales).

- If you plan on traveling for interviews or to scope out other cities, download these apps to your phone: Uber, TripIt, Airbnb, and your airline's app.

- Download Audible if your library does not check out audiobooks or if you want a larger selection.

- Download a book pertaining to finding a job, self-development, leadership, or your industry.

- Use Siri/Google Now to set a reminder once a month to download a new Audible book.

- Go to your local library's website. Do they have audiobook rental options with OverDrive?

- If your library uses OverDrive, download it.

- Reserve or check out a book pertaining to finding a job, personal development, leadership or your industry.

- If you have iOS and are using Evernote, download Scannable if you'd like the ability to scan documents to send to potential employers.

- Download the Facebook app.

- Create a strong Facebook profile that shows your personality, but really illustrates your professionalism.

- On Facebook, send individual friend requests to key contacts with a message stating that, if they connect with professional contacts on Facebook, you would love to be connected.

- Once a week, communicate with key contacts who are on Facebook. Comment on a new picture, send an article of interest based on their posts, etc.

- Join a professional group or local networking group on Facebook.

- If you're using Facebook, download the separate Messenger app to communicate with Facebook friends about job opportunities one-on-one.

- Download the Nextdoor app or visit the website and create a profile.

- Reach out to neighbors via Nextdoor asking about business or career opportunities. Be specific with your areas of expertise and provide a link to your resume or LinkedIn profile.

- Download the LinkedIn app.

- Update/create your LinkedIn profile. Include a professional photo, full summary, past work experiences, educational history, etc. Fill it out completely. Note: this will be easier to do from a PC.

- Add your business connections to LinkedIn with connection requests.

- Join professional LinkedIn groups and other groups likely to contain hiring managers in your industry.

- Upgrade to LinkedIn Premium for upgraded job-finding features.

- Tell your intelligent assistant to "Set Daily Reminder" to check LinkedIn messages at <insert time>.

- Use Fiverr or Upwork to hire someone to design your resume, edit or proof your resume, or create a cover letter. If you're in a creative industry, look at "infographic resumes" as an option as well.

- Use Fiverr or Upwork to hire someone to design custom social media headers and/or backgrounds.

- Download Google Drive and Google Docs for document sharing and storage.

- Upload your resume and cover letter to Google Drive in order to always have access to it whenever someone requests it.

- Send share links or invite trusted professionals or connections to comment and edit your resume/cover letter in Google Docs.

- Give people helping you with your resume the link to edit your resume/cover letter in Google Docs. Make sure you check the permissions to ensure they can edit versus just viewing!

- Download Google Maps for mapping how to get to interviews and networking events.

- Download Hangouts for video chats with potential employers in another city, career coaches, etc.

- Create a folder in Evernote or OneNote called "Daily To-Do List." Create your first note in it with today's date. And put in to-do items regarding your job search using the checklist feature. You can also use ToDoIst for daily to-do items; however, I find Evernote or OneNote faster.

- To manage short- and long-term to-do lists, download ToDoIst.

- Create a ToDoIst list called Job Search. Add to-do items including items such as revise resume, send resume to three companies, follow up with Mike on open positions at his company, buy a new suit for interviews, book flight for interview on June 24, etc.

- Add StayFocusd or SelfControl to your browser.

- Download the YouTube app.

- Consider creating a video resume and uploading it to YouTube.

- Follow your prospective employers' YouTube channels to keep up with company developments.

- Sign up to drive Uber for extra spending money.

- Sign up to deliver Postmates for extra spending money.

- Download Airbnb and list a room in your home for extra spending money.

- Create an account in IFTTT.

- In IFTTT type the following in the search box: Get an email for new Craigslist listings. Open a new window and go to Craiglist. Find the job category you're interested in. Copy the URL from the top of the page and then paste that into the IFTTT recipe (e.g., for Houston accounting jobs, the URL is https://houston.craigslist.org/search/acc).

- In IFTTT type the following in the search box: Create a daily email digest of new articles from The NYTimes Job Market section. Confirm.

- Sign up for SendOutCards to send custom cards to contacts.

- Send a custom SendOutCard (and possibly small gift card) to contacts who refer or provide leads.

- Send a SendOutCard to interviewers.

- _____

  _____

- _____

  _____

Build Better Business Connections

- Sign up for Shoeboxed.

- Put all loose business cards into a Shoeboxed envelope and mail them off.

- Upload Shoeboxed contacts into LinkedIn and send them a connection request.

- Download the Evernote or OneNote Web app to your phone.

- Download the Evernote or OneNote Web Clipper to your browser.

- Create the following folders in Evernote or OneNote: Professional

Items of Interest, Industry News, and Networking Talking Points.

- Add StayFocusd or SelfControl to your browser.

- Use FaceTime to catch up with less formal contacts.

- Create a Twitter list named "Networking Groups."

- Add five organizations or associations to your "Networking Groups" Twitter list.

- Create a Twitter list for all of your industry news sources.

- Use Siri/Google Now to set a reminder once a day to check your "Networking Groups" Twitter list.

- If you plan on traveling for networking events or conventions in other cities, download these apps to your phone: Uber, TripIt, Airbnb, and your airline's app.

- Download Groupon.

- Buy a Groupon to a favorite or cool restaurant you'd like to try with contacts.

- Download Google Translate if you have international contacts who may post on social media or use sayings from their native language.

- Set up a Google Alert for the name of prominent contacts in order to know when they win awards/get promotions, etc. Call them/email them/send a card when they have a new accomplishment.

- Set up a Google Alert for industry items of interest that you should be knowledgeable about in a conversation with peers.

- Download Grammarly to your browser for additional protection for error-free online communication.

- Download Audible if your library does not check out audiobooks or if you want a larger selection.

- Download a book pertaining to networking, to your industry, or that will give you interesting items to talk about at events or with contacts.

- Use Siri/Google Now to set a reminder once a month to download a new Audible book.

- Go to your local library's website. Do they have audiobook rental options with OverDrive?

- If your library uses OverDrive, download it.

- Via your library's website, reserve or check out an audiobook pertaining to networking, to your industry, or that will give you interesting items to talk about at events or with contacts.

- Download the Facebook app.

- Create a strong Facebook profile that shows your personality, but really illustrates your professionalism.

- Send a new contact whom you just met a Facebook friend request.

- On Facebook, send individual friend requests to key contacts with a message stating that, if they connect with professional contacts on Facebook, you would love to be connected.

- Once a week, communicate with key contacts who are on Facebook. Comment on a new picture, send an article of interest based on their posts, etc.

- Join a professional group or local networking group on Facebook.

- If you're using Facebook, download the separate Messenger app to communicate with Facebook friends one-on-one.

- Download Nextdoor.com and create a profile.

- Reach out to neighbors asking about job opportunities. Be specific with your areas of expertise and provide a link to your resume or LinkedIn profile.

- Download the LinkedIn app.

- Create a strong LinkedIn profile. Include a professional photo, full summary, past work experiences, educational history, etc. Fill it out completely. Note: this will be easiest to do from a PC.

- Add your business connections through LinkedIn connection requests.

- Add a new contact, whom you just met through a LinkedIn connection request.

- Join professional LinkedIn groups and other groups likely to contain hiring managers in your industry.

- Send a message to "catch up" with a LinkedIn connection that you have not lately interacted with.

- Tell your intelligent assistant to "Set Daily Reminder" to check LinkedIn messages at <insert time>.

- Use Fiverr or Upwork to hire someone to design custom social media headers and/or backgrounds.

- Download Google Maps for directions on how to get to networking events.

- Download Hangouts for video chats with contacts who don't live near you.

- Schedule "coffee" with a connection and enjoy a digital coffee meeting with them via Hangouts.

- Create a folder in Evernote or OneNote called "Daily To-Do List." Create your first note in it with today's date. Put in to-do items regarding following up and/or checking in with connections. You can also use ToDoIst for daily to-do items; however, I find Evernote or OneNote faster.

- To manage short- and long-term to-do lists, download ToDoIst.

- Create a ToDoIst list called Networking. Add to-do items including items like revise LinkedIn profile, send item of interest to three influencers, follow up with Shelley Jones on her new raise, buy a new suit for convention, book flight for convention on June 24, etc.

- Add StayFocusd or SelfControl to your browser.

- Follow your prospective employers' channels to keep up with company developments.

- Download TripAdvisor.

- Download OpenTable.

- Use TripAdvisor or OpenTable to find a restaurant or venue to meet up with a business contact.

- Make a reservation for a business meet-up using OpenTable.

- Create a Facebook list of your key contacts.

- Add the Evernote app to your mobile device and upgrade to Premium for card-scanning abilities.

- Scan the business cards from a recent event using Evernote and tap the option to automatically send them a LinkedIn connection request.

- Schedule a special birthday for a key client/influencer using Fiverr—e.g., if they love Disney, get a puppeteer to create a video of Disney puppets singing happy birthday.

- Tell your intelligent assistant to "Set Daily Reminder" to check LinkedIn messages at <insert time>.

- Create a folder in Evernote or OneNote called "Daily To-Do List." Create your first note in it with today's date. And put in to-do items regarding connections using the checklist feature.

- Go to Doodle.com to schedule a meeting with contacts. Put in a few dates/time options (I recommend 3–4) and send out to participant(s).

- Create an account in IFTTT.

- Click on the Browse tab in IFTTT. Activate one recipe that will streamline your networking process.

- Create an account in Zapier.

- Click on the Explore tab in Zapier. Activate one recipe that will streamline your networking process.

- Sign up for SendOutCards to send custom cards to contacts.

- Send a custom SendOutCard (and possibly small gift card) to contacts with recent accomplishments, to reestablish connection, etc.

- _____
  _____

- _____
  _____

- _____
  _____

- _____
  _____

- _____
  _____

Get Clients

- Sign up for Shoeboxed.

- Put all loose business cards into a Shoeboxed envelope and mail them.

- Upload Shoeboxed contacts into LinkedIn and send them a connection request.

- Download the Evernote or OneNote Web app to your phone.

- Download the Evernote or OneNote Web Clipper to your browser.

- Create the following folders in Evernote or OneNote: Professional Items of Interest, Industry News, Key Clients, and Prospects.

- Add StayFocusd or SelfControl to your browser.

- Create Twitter lists named "Key Clients" and "Prospects."

- Add five organizations or associations to each Twitter list.

- Download Google Drive and Google Docs.

- Use Google Drive and Google Docs to collaborate with current clients and prospects on existing and future projects.

- Download Google Translate if you have international contacts who may post on social media or use sayings from their native language.

- Download Grammarly to your browser for additional protection for error-free online communication.

- Use Siri/Google Now to set a reminder once a day to check your Twitter lists.

- If you plan on traveling to other cities for client meetings download these apps to your phone: Uber, TripIt, Airbnb, and your airline's app.

- Download Audible if your library does not check out audiobooks or if you want a larger selection.

- Download a book pertaining to networking, to your industry, or that will give you interesting items to talk about at events or with contacts.

- Use Siri/Google Now to set a reminder once a month to download a new Audible book.

- Go to your local library's website. Do they have audiobook rental options with OverDrive?

- If your library uses OverDrive, download it.

- Via your library's website, reserve or check out a book pertaining to networking, to your industry, or that will give you interesting items to talk about at events or with contacts.

- Download the Facebook app.

- Create a strong Facebook profile that shows your personality, but really illustrates your professionalism.

- Send a new contact whom you just met a Facebook friend request.

- On Facebook, send individual friend requests to key contacts with a message stating that, if they connect with professional contacts on Facebook, you would love to be connected.

- Create Facebook lists for Clients and Prospects. Add Contacts to the lists.

- Once a week, communicate with clients, prospects, and referral partners who are on Facebook. Comment on a new picture, send an article of interest based on their posts, etc.

- Join a professional group or local networking group on Facebook.

- If you're using Facebook, download the separate Messenger app to communicate with Facebook friends one-on-one.

- Set up Google Alerts for the names of your key clients and prospects in order to know when they win awards/get promotions, etc.

- Call them/email them/send a card when they have a new accomplishment.

- Set up a Google Alert for industry items of interest that you should be knowledgeable about in a conversation with clients/prospects.

- Download the Nextdoor app and create a profile.

- Reach out to neighbors via Nextdoor when they express a need that fits into your offerings.

- Download the LinkedIn app.

- Add your business connections through LinkedIn connection requests.

- Add a new contact, whom you just met, through a LinkedIn connection request.

- Join professional LinkedIn groups and other groups likely to contain hiring managers in your industry.

- Send a message to "catch up" with a LinkedIn connection with whom you have not lately interacted.

- Tell your intelligent assistant to "Set Daily Reminder" to check LinkedIn messages at <insert time>.

- Use Fiverr or Upwork to hire someone to design custom social media headers and/or backgrounds.

- Hire someone from Upwork to take your draft client presentation and turn it into a polished slideshow.

- Download Google Maps and use for directions to meetings.

- Download Hangouts for video chats with prospects, clients, and referral partners.

- Schedule "coffee" with a referral partner and enjoy a digital coffee meeting with them via Hangouts.

- Create a folder in Evernote or OneNote called "Daily To-Do List." Create your first note in it with today's date. And add to-do items regarding following up and/or checking in with connections. You can also use ToDoIst for daily to-do items; however, I find Evernote or OneNote faster.

- To manage short- and long-term to-do lists, download ToDoIst.

- Create a ToDoIst list called "Networking." Add to-do items including items like revise LinkedIn profile, send item of interest to three influencers, follow up with Shelley Jones on her new raise, buy a new suit for convention, book flight for convention on June 24, etc.

- Add StayFocusd or SelfControl to your browser.

- Go to Doodle.com to schedule a meeting with clients/prospects. Put in a few dates/time options (I recommend 3–4) and send out to participant(s).

- Download Scannable to easily scan and send documents to current and prospective clients on the go.

- Follow your prospective clients' YouTube channels to keep up with company developments.

- Download TripAdvisor.

- Download OpenTable.

- Use TripAdvisor or OpenTable to find a restaurant or venue to meet up with a business contact. Use OpenTable to make reservations.

- Add the Evernote app to your mobile device and upgrade to Premium for card-scanning abilities.

- Scan the business cards from a recent event using Evernote, and tap the option to automatically send them a LinkedIn connection request.

- Schedule a special birthday for a key client/influencer using Fiverr—e.g., if they love Disney, get a puppeteer to create a video of Disney puppets singing happy birthday.

- Tell your intelligent assistant to "Set Daily Reminder" to check LinkedIn messages at <insert time>.

- Create a folder in Evernote or OneNote called "Daily To-Do List."

- Create your first note in it with today's date, and add to-do items regarding connections using the checklist feature.

- Sign up for Square at squareup.com.

- Download Square register.

- Create an account in IFTTT.

- Click on the Browse tab in IFTTT. Activate one recipe that will help you strengthen client relationships and stay in contact with prospects.

- Create an account in Zapier.

- Click on the Explore tab in Zapier. Activate one recipe that will help you strengthen client relationships and stay in contact with prospects.

- Sign up for SendOutCards to send custom cards to contacts.

- Send a custom SendOutCard (and possibly small gift card) to contacts after meetings or as a congratulations.

- _____

  _____

- _____

  _____

- _____

  _____

- _____

  _____

Improve/Organize Home Life

- Download the Evernote or OneNote Web app to your phone.

- Download the Evernote or OneNote Web Clipper to your browser.

- Create the following folders in Evernote or OneNote: Manuals, Home Projects, and Activities. Feel free to add additional folders.

- Download Scannable.

- Using Scannable, scan all of your manuals, house-related receipts, recipes, etc., and save them in Evernote or upload to OneNote or Google Drive.

- Upload/keep home information (e.g., manuals, home dimensions, blueprint) in your Google Drive folder.

- Download Out of Milk or Instacart to your phone.

- Download Out of Milk or Instacart to all the phones in your household, and sync with your account.

- Create store lists in Out of Milk.

- Add your grocery list to Out of Milk.

- Sign up for recurring air filter delivery.

- Sign up for recurring refrigerator water filter delivery.

- Don't want to have to think about what to cook for each meal or shop for groceries? Download the Blue Apron app and sign up for a plan.

- Download the Fancy Hands app and sign up for a plan.

- Delegate one item (e.g., finding orange and green girl's socks, making a doctor's appointment, research top five steak restaurants in Orlando) to a Fancy Hands assistant.

- Download the Postmates app.

- Order dinner/home party catering from a restaurant without a delivery service.

- Order important forgotten items when in a bind. E.g., kids' dress socks two hours before an event starts, first aid kit 90 minutes before it's time to leave for a camping trip.

- Download the Evernote Web Clipper to your browser.

- Download the OneNote Web Clipper to your browser.

- Add StayFocusd or SelfControl to your browser.

- Download your bank's app. Answer the following questions: Do I see where to transfer money? Do I see how to cash a check? What is the limit on cashing checks?

- Download your airline's app if you have any upcoming flights.

- Download your hospital or pharmacy app if you have regular prescriptions or visit your doctor more than once per year.

- Download Uber.

- Outsource a project like furniture assembly or house painting using TaskRabbit.

- Download Airbnb.

- Download Nextdoor.com and create a profile.

- Give something away on Nextdoor.

- Order groceries using Instacart.

- Ask the neighborhood for a recommendation for a professional service (healthcare, carpet cleaning, restaurant, etc.).

- Find someone to clean your home using TaskRabbit.

- Hire a handyman to take care of all of your honey-do items using TaskRabbit.

- Create a folder in Evernote or OneNote called "Daily To-Do List." Create your first note in it with today's date, and add to-do items using the checklist feature.

- Using Siri, Cortana, or Google Now create a new note in Evernote. In the note, list all of the things you need to do that you haven't done. List all of the things that you want to do to feel caught up.

- Purchase household items (e.g., mop, cookbook, electronics) using Amazon instead of going to individual stores. Prime members get free 2-day delivery and non-members are also eligible for free delivery on some items.

- To manage short- and long-term to-do lists, download ToDoIst.

- Create a ToDoIst list called Home Projects. Add to-do items including items such as find cleaning service, interview contractors, buy paint for living room, etc.

- Download the YouTube app.

- Use YouTube for a how-to video (e.g., recipe, staining furniture, etc.)

- Create an account in IFTTT.

- Click on the Channels tab in IFTTT and choose Craigslist. Set up a recipe to receive an email or text when an item you are interested in is mentioned on Craigslist.

- Go to IFTTT and type "home" in the search box to find a list of additional recipes for home automation.

- If you're in the market for new electronics or home materials, view the Best Buy and Home Depot recipes in IFTTT that will alert you when prices drop on items of interest.

- _____

  _____

- _____

  _____

- _____

  _____

- _____

  _____

Personal Development

- Download the Evernote or OneNote Web app to your phone.

- Download the Evernote or OneNote Web Clipper to your browser.

- Create the following folders in Evernote or OneNote based on areas you want to improve or sharpen. Examples include: Book List, Makeover, Classes.

- Using Siri, Cortana, or Google Now create a new note in Evernote. In the note, list all of the things you'd like to do/know to become your ideal you.

- Add StayFocusd or SelfControl to your browser to minimize time spent on distracting websites.

- Add sites like Facebook and Pinterest to StayFocusd or SelfControl to limit the amount of time you spend there.

- Download Audible and sign up for a subscription.

- Download an audiobook from Audible that will help you accomplish your personal development goals.

- Go to your local library's website. Do they have audiobook rental options with OverDrive? If so, download OverDrive.

- Using your intelligent assistant, set a reminder every month to download a new book on Audible.

- Download/use Google Maps to map out directions to appointments at the beginning of the day to give you an idea of how early you should leave to **arrive five to ten minutes early**. Adjust for normal traffic conditions (e.g., rush hour).

- Download Google Translate to help you learn new languages. This is especially helpful if you're taking a course to get involved in a language exchange program.

- Download Groupon and create an account.

- Search Groupon for discount classes on topics of interest (e.g., archery, language, exercise).

- Download Google Hangouts.

- Use Google Hangouts for one-on-one tutoring sessions with a professional.

- Download the LinkedIn app.

- Join LinkedIn industry groups.

- Use Siri/Google Now to set a reminder twice a week to check your LinkedIn groups for interesting articles/information.

- Under Interests on LinkedIn, check out SlideShare and Learning (Lydia subscription) to stay abreast of information and learn skills.

- To manage short- and long-term to-do lists, download ToDoIst.

- Create a ToDoIst list called Personal Development. Add to-do items including items such as buy a language course, buy three new suits, subscribe to three periodicals, etc.

- Download the Twitter app.

- Create a Twitter list named Industry News and add five industry-based accounts to the list.

- Create a Twitter list to follow experts of interest to you. Add five experts.

- Download the YouTube app.

- Watch a how-to video aimed at helping you develop a skill.

- For reputation management purposes, create a Google Alert for your name, if it isn't common.

- _____

  _____

- _____

  _____

- _____

  _____

Plan and Enjoy Free Time

- If you're looking for vacation (or staycation) housing, download the Airbnb app.

- If you have purchased airline tickets, download your airline's app.

- Download the Amazon app to purchase things: books, specialty soaps, instruments, and more. If you plan on buying things throughout the year, consider Amazon Prime membership for free shipping and access to additional benefits.

- Download Audible and sign up for a subscription.

- Download an audiobook from Audible just for fun.

- Do you enjoy cooking? Download the Blue Apron app and sign up for a plan.

- Download the Evernote or OneNote app to your phone.

- Download the Evernote Web Clipper to your browser or download the OneNote Web Clipper to your browser.

- Create any of the following folders in Evernote or OneNote:

Vacation Ideas, Book List, Bucket List, My Favorite Places, Restaurants I Want to Try.

- Buy a Groupon to a favorite or cool restaurant you'd like to try.

- Buy a Groupon for a fun activity like painting or paintball.

- Go to your local library's website. Do they have audiobook rental options with OverDrive? If so, download OverDrive.

- Check out an OverDrive book.

- Download TripAdvisor for restaurant and entertainment options.

- Use TripAdvisor to find a fun activity or event.

- Download OpenTable.

- Make a reservation for yourself at a nice restaurant using OpenTable.

- Download Tripit if you're planning any trips.

- Forward all confirmation emails (from hotel, airlines, etc.) to TripAdvisor in order to create a single itinerary.

- Need taxi/car service to get around? Download Uber and set up your profile.

- Set up a Google Alert for items that matter to your family or group of friends (e.g., cancer trials, travel destinations) and forward information as you receive it.

- Add StayFocusd or SelfControl to your browser to help free up more time to spend with family.

- Add websites to StayFocusd or SelfControl, such as Facebook, Twitter, etc.

- _____

  _____

- _____

  _____

- _____

  _____

Self-Care in the Technology Age

Not long ago I assisted my husband, an international photographer, with a very large family shoot. There were nearly thirty people, ranging in age from three to over seventy-five. In between shots and staging, instead of talking to each other, a full 75% of them pulled out smartphones and began pecking away.

Weeks after the above event, my husband suggested we invite family members to watch fireworks. As we sat in beach chairs in a parking lot with hundreds of other families, waiting for the festivities to begin, I noted that over half of the people were on their phones.

While the examples above would not faze many other Millennials or people of any age, this observation sat heavy on my spirit. I love technology because I understand that it has given us new opportunities and resources. At the same time, I lament the loss of more personal forms of communication. Technology does not replace face-to-face interaction, phone calls, or handwritten notes. The trick is to use technology versus being used by it.

Enjoy a Digital Detox

If you're feeling overwhelmed because you find yourself checking your phone constantly, or if you are hearing the phone ring when it isn't, or if you just need a break, consider a "digital detox." It can be for a few hours or even a few days. You define what will work for you.

When I take a detox, I tell my husband that I'll be gone until a certain time (later that day or the next day). If I'm renting a beach house or other accommodations, I give him that information as well. On the day of my detox, I turn off my phone—yes, you read that correctly; I turn off my phone—and commit to no television, radio, computer, Internet, or smart-phone. From there, I either get in my silent (no radio playing) car and drive to my accommodations (directions to which I would have printed out the day prior) or jump in my car and start driving, with specific or no destinations in mind. I've visited my local Buddhist Temple, thrift book-store, and favorite restaurant. I might get a massage or sit in the park or at the beach reading a physical book. The point is to shut out all of the chatter that living a life constantly connected to technology can create. When I return, I'm always revitalized and better able to use technology as a tool versus a compulsion.

If my method is too extreme or not extensive enough for you, create your own! Maybe you need a week's vacation at a ranch. Perhaps, you cannot completely turn off your phone because you're a parent. However, you can turn off all calls except from specific numbers and alert your family that you should only be contacted if there is a legitimate medical emergency. Maybe cutting off all the forms of technology I suggested seems like too much. No worries! Maybe just take a break from your smartphone, social media, and the web. Do what works for you!

Like a computer, when we hit the reset button, we are able to have a new start working with greater effectiveness!

Start a Smartphone Diet

If you're trying to curb your habits, a smartphone diet may be more to your liking. Maybe you want to spend less time on your smartphone in between necessary usage. In this case, choose to not pick up your phone whenever you are bored or waiting for someone or something to happen. Instead, pick up a physical book (not the e-book on your phone, that's cheating). Inform your friends and family of your new diet, so they can kindly help urge you to put your phone down when you're resorting to old habits. While having certain apps on your phone can be helpful, bad habits with these apps can suck efficiency. If you're finding yourself constantly checking various accounts or even hearing notifications when there are none, try one or more of the following solutions:

- Turn off notifications from social networks with the possible exception of LinkedIn.

- Remove the Facebook app from your phone.

- Remove the Facebook Messenger app from your phone.

- Remove additional time-suck apps from your phone.

Set Boundaries

Every technology user should have boundaries. These are rules developed to help you stay focused on the things that really matter to you. Pick the following boundaries that work for you:

- I will not look at my phone before bed or after 9:00 p.m.

- I will not sleep with my smartphone in my room. I will use an alarm clock to wake up.

- I will put my phone away at family gatherings.

- I will not look at my phone at social gatherings.

- I will only allow myself to take up to ____ pictures per day, in order to be fully present (in the moment) at places or events.

- I will not post pictures of myself with the following people or in the following places:

I would also encourage you to respect other people's boundaries. For instance, I frequently ask my five-year-old nephew for permission before posting pictures of him online. Often he feels very comfortable agreeing to the posting, but sometimes he tells me that I may not post his picture. I also have loved ones who have requested that no friends or family members post their images online. I respect their wishes, and, when posting the rare family photo in a secret Facebook family history group, I put a dot over their faces.

Finding It Hard to Power Off?

If you find it hard to put your phone down or power off your tablet or laptop, keep the following in mind:

- Chances are extremely slim that you'll miss anything extremely important.

- You're not as important as you think you are. This may seem harsh, but if any one of us dies tomorrow, those we love will find a way to carry on, our coworkers will manage, and the earth will continue spinning on its axis.

- The more time you spend away from your smartphone, the more strategic you will be when you do use it. Your actions will not be compulsive, but decisive!

- Your family and friends deserve your undistracted attention.

- Smartphones can be a distraction from our intuition, conscience, and inner voice. You might be missing out on important things you're drawn to do!

Putting It All Together

It may take a little time for you to become accustomed to using apps, extensions, and websites to fill those gaps in your busy life. However, with time, you'll become a pro at leaning on technology. For instance, I recently found myself needing to complete several different chores around 6:00 p.m. I needed to finish writing a chapter of this book, workout, purchase groceries, cook dinner, and pick up a few items from Home Depot. I obviously could not complete all of those tasks, or could I? I opened the Instacart app and scheduled groceries to be delivered at 8:00 p.m. While driving to the gym, I used the text-to-voice feature in Evernote to dictate the rest of the chapter. When I returned home, just prior to taking a shower, I ordered dinner and the items needed from Home Depot using the Postmates app. **I completed every single item on my to-do list and made time for self-care in the form of exercise!**

Use technology to gift yourself with more sleep, better eating habits, time at the gym, and general peace of mind. You are worth it!

Easy Reference Apps Chart

APP	👥	💲	⚭	🤝	🏠	🧑	🌅
Airbnb	●	●		●		●	●
Airline Apps	●	●		●		●	●
Amazon	●				●	●	●
Audible		●	●		●	●	
Banking Apps				●			
Blue Apron	●				●		●
Evernote	●	●	●	●	●	●	●
Facebook	●	●	●	●		●	
FaceTime	●		●				●
Fancy Hands				●			
Fiverr	●	●	●	●			
Google Docs	●	●	●	●			
Google Drive	●	●		●	●		
Google Maps	●	●	●	●		●	
Google Translate	●		●	●		●	
Groupon	●		●			●	●
Hangouts	●	●	●	●		●	
Hospital Apps				●			
Instacart				●			

APP	👥	💵	✳️	🤝	🏠	👤	🌅
LinkedIn		●	●	●		●	
Messenger (Facebook)	●	●	●	●			
Nextdoor	●	●		●	●		
OneNote	●	●	●	●	●	●	●
OpenTable	●		●	●			●
Out of Milk				●			
OverDrive					●	●	
Pharmacy Apps				●			
Postmates				●			
Scannable		●		●	●		
Square Register				●			
TaskRabbit				●			
ToDoIst	●	●	●	●	●	●	
TripAdvisor	●		●	●			●
TripIt	●	●	●	●			●
Twitter		●	●	●		●	
Uber		●		●			
Upwork		●		●			
YouTube		●		●	●	●	
Zoom	●						

Easy Reference Browser Extension Chart

APP	👥	💵	⚛	🤝	🏠	🧑	🌅
Evernote Web Clipper	●	●	●	●	●	●	●
Honey					●		
Grammarly		●	●	●			
OneNote Web Clipper	●	●	●	●	●	●	●
SelfControl		●	●	●			
StayFocusd		●	●	●			

Additional Resources

Now you understand the practical applications of social media, apps, and extensions. You've already downloaded efficiency apps, started taking some new steps with social media to aid in relationship-building, and downloaded some helpful extensions to your browser. You may want to look at some more in-depth resources to take a deeper dive into some of the items mentioned. Below are just a few of my favorite books and blogs on the subject.

Blogs and Websites

http://www.cnet.com/
http://www.makeuseof.com/
https://techcrunch.com/
http://www.zdnet.com/

Books

Barton, Matthew. *Evernote: Discover The Life Changing Power of Evernote. Quick Start Guide To Improve Your Productivity And Get Things Done At Lightning Speed! CreateSpace Independent Publishing Platform*, 2016.

Downey, Alex. *OneNote: The Ultimate Guide to OneNote – Goals, Time Management & Productivity*. CreateSpace Independent Publishing Platform, 2016.

Hughes, Bill. *Samsung Galaxy S7 For Dummies*. Hoboken, NJ: John Wiley & Sons, Inc., 2016.*

Muir, Nancy C. *iPhone For Seniors For Dummies, 5th Edition*. Hoboken, NJ: John Wiley & Sons, Inc., 2016.

Ziesenis, Beth. *Nerd Know-How: The 27+ Best Apps for Work & How to Use 'Em!* San Diego, CA: Avenue Z, Inc., 2015.

---

*For Dummies has versions of this book for each past version of Samsung as well as other Android devices.

Glossary

In this section, you will find a list of social media related terms used in this book.

#. A symbol appearing at the beginning of a hashtag on Twitter and Google+; used to find posts about specific topics.

@. A symbol used to tag another social media user on a social network that turns their name into a link to their profile while alerting them to view the post.

Airbnb. An online marketplace that enables people to list, find, and rent vacation homes.

Amazon. The world's largest online retailer that also offers cloud storage.

App Store. Apple's resource for downloading music, movies, games, and other apps to iOS devices.

Audible. The world's largest producer of audiobooks with books available by subscription.

Blue Apron. A food subscription service that delivers pre-portioned meal ingredients with recipes.

Blog. A website where a single user or multiple users share experiences, content, or other information, normally centered on a specific topic or theme.

Browser. A program that provides a way to find, read, and interact with all the information on the World Wide Web.

Comments. Responses left by other users on a social media post.

Cortana. Window's intelligent assistant which performs tasks for its user.

Cloud. A network of remote servers hosted on the Internet—rather than a local server or personal computer—to store, manage, and process data.

Doodle. A scheduling polling service that enables users to identify the best times to meet for participants.

Extension. A piece of technology that allows a web browser—like Safari or Chrome—to perform additional actions.

Evernote. An app that allows end users to capture, store, and synchronize text, images, video files, etc., across computing devices.

Evernote Web Clipper. An extension that enables users to capture full-page articles, selected text, images, important emails, and web pages.

Facebook. A social network, with over one billion users, that allows users to post pictures, create posts, send private messages, participate in groups, and much more.

FaceTime. An Apple application that allows users with front-facing cameras to video chat over the Internet.

Fancy Hands. A team of U.S.-based assistants accessible by any device at any time of the day.

Feed. A constantly updating list of posts from your connections on social media sites.

Follow. The ability to see posts from a social media user on social networks; the user may or may not elect to see your posts.

Fiverr. A global online marketplace offering tasks and services starting at a cost of $5 per job.

Friend. A social media connection.

Google Alerts. A free service from Google that notifies users via email when content (e.g., news articles, blogs, web pages) are added to the web that matches words or terms the user is following

Google Docs. A free application that allows users to create, edit, and store documents and spreadsheets online.

Google Drive. A personal cloud storage service from Google that enables users to store and synchronize content across computers, laptops, and mobile devices.

Google Maps. A web-based service that provides detailed information about geographical regions and sites around the world, including directions for driving, walking, riding public transportation, or biking; it also includes road maps for aerial and satellite views.

Google Now. Google's Android intelligent assistant that performs tasks for its user.

Google Translate. A free web-based program, extension, and app that instantly translates words, phrases, voice, and web pages in over 100 languages.

Grammarly. An online grammar checker with a computer browser extension.

Group. A type of private or public page created in social networks like Facebook, LinkedIn, and Google+ that users can join based on a common interest or affiliation; users can communicate with other group members.

Groupon. An e-commerce service that features significant deals from local merchants on items including travel, goods, activities, and services.

Hangouts. (Google Hangouts) A communications service—available on both Android and iOS—that allows members to initiate and participate by text, voice, or video chats, both one-on-one or in a group.

Hashtag. A word starting with the symbol "#" on social networks; used to find posts about specific topics.

Honey. An extension that automatically applies the best working coupon codes to online shopping cart orders that customers are already receiving at a discount.

If This Then That (IFTTT). An extremely powerful efficiency and automation program that enables users to leverage "recipes" to create chains of simple conditional statements, which are triggered based on changes to other web services such as Gmail or Facebook.

Instacart. A grocery delivery app.

Intelligent Assistants. Software agents with the ability to perform tasks for its user.

Like. The action of clicking a button on a social network, indicating that you agree, enjoy, or have seen a post or comment.

LinkedIn. A social network dedicated to professional interactions with more than 200 million users.

Messenger. Facebook's app for individual person-to-person and group messaging.

Mobile App. Software designed to run on smartphones, tablets, and other mobile devices that are generally created to allow users similar experiences as if accessing a PC, but often with more limited functions.

Nextdoor. A private social network just for you and your neighbors.

OneNote. An app that allows end users to capture, store, and synchronize text, images, video files, etc., across computing devices.

OneNote Web Clipper. A browser extension that enables users to save websites or pieces of information from the web.

OpenTable. A free app for online reservations creation, restaurant reviews, and loyalty points toward free meals.

Out of Milk. A simple-to-use shopping list app that synchronizes among multiple devices and users.

OverDrive. A service app that enables users to borrow e-books, audio-books, and more from their local public libraries.

Page. A profile specifically for businesses, organizations, and brands on social networks.

Play Store. Andoid's resource for downloading music, movies, games, and other apps to Android devices.

Post. A social media update; can contain text, images, photos, and/or video.

Postmates. A delivery service app whose contractors will deliver items from restaurants and shops that typically do not offer delivery as an option.

Profile. The place where a single social media user's information, photos, posts, etc., appear on a social network; has its own unique URL.

RSS. Short for Rich Site Summary or Really Simple Syndication; a content delivery system used to publish frequently updated websites that allows readers to receive updates of new posts.

Scannable. A scanning application that enables users to scan individual or multi-page documents using their phone camera that they can then store in Evernote or send via email.

SelfControl. A Safari extension that limits the amount of time users can spend on distracting websites.

Sendoutcards. A custom card and gift delivery service.

Share. The act of reposting another user's post; can be a text, photo, article, or video.

Shoeboxed.com. A service that, for a monthly fee, scans large and small quantities of business cards and receipts for users who can then download the information or create reports.

Siri. Apple's intelligent assistant that performs tasks for its user.

Social Media. Websites that allow users to connect with each other based on shared interests and mutual connections.

Social Networks. Social media that allows users to create profiles and build relationships.

Square Register. An app that allows users to accept debit or credit cards anywhere, right from their phone.

StayFocusd. A Chrome extension that limits the amount of time users can spend on distracting websites.

Tag. The ability to mention another social media user, making their name a link to their own profile, using the "@" sign.

TaskRabbit. An online and mobile marketplace that matches freelance labor with local demand, allowing consumers to find immediate help with tasks like cleaning and handyman items.

Thumbtack. An online and mobile marketplace that matches freelance labor with local demand, allowing consumers to find immediate help with tasks like personal training and home painting.

Timeline. A user's profile on Facebook; it is called a Tweet on Twitter.

TripAdvisor. A website built around travel that assists customers in gathering travel information, posting reviews, and engaging in travel forums.

TripIt. A service that organizes all travel plans in one place.

Todoist. A personal and professional project management app.

Twitter. A social network that allows users to quickly and concisely (140 characters or less) express things important to them, where they can connect with other people who value the same things.

Uber. An app that enables users to book transportation on the spot; similar to hiring a taxi or car service.

Upwork. A service that allows users to hire contractors from all over the world to perform creative and administrative tasks.

YouTube. A social network that allows users to share, comment on, and perform minor editing of videos.

Zapier. An automation service that enables users to automate actions connecting separate business services using "zaps," without any coding.

Zoom. A high definition video-conferencing and desktop-sharing software that has both an app and browser extension.

Acknowledgements

The making of this book was truly a community effort. I am forever grateful to the team of people who contributed their talents in the form of ideas, time, suggestions, corrections, and encouragement.

Thank you to my super husband, CJ Martin, for his constant support, encouragement, and patience. Sir, you are the Ricky to my Lucy! Thank you to my entire family for encouraging me to be curious, to strive for excellence, and, most important, to be kind and seek ways to be of service to others. Thank you to Bambi McCullough for offering up your lovely home as a writing retreat for this book and a special thanks to Hitaji Aziz for providing support. Thank you to my fabulous super-assistant Regina Baker whose constant aid made this book possible. Thank you to my book coach Nekisha Michelle for keeping me on track during the writing process. Thank you Craig Price and the National Speakers Association for all of your assistance in recommending resources.

I am eternally grateful to my wonderful volunteer book assassins, recruited from Facebook, whose contributions and hard work surpassed anything I expected and whose wonderful suggestions reshaped many parts of this book. Thank you Sherea Cary, Terri Craig, Edward Rose III,

Dr. Taffy Wagner, and Kimyon Zari.

Thank you to my editor, Joyous Seeman, for another wonderful project together. Thank you to my audience members, clients, and social media friends who selected the cover for this book and supported me throughout the writing process.

About the Author

When powerful companies want their teams to take action online, they book social media expert and dynamic speaker Crystal Washington, who has worked with Google, Microsoft, GE, and others in the USA, Africa, and Europe. For this comprehensive knowledge on social media, she has been interviewed by ABC, NBC, FOX, CBS, and numerous radio stations and magazines around the globe.

Crystal is well known for her ability to take complex web and social media topics, and make them easy to understand and accessible for everyday people and small business owners. She owns CWM Enterprises, a social media instructional brand aimed at training everyone from Gen Ys to Baby Boomers in strategically using social media. Her passion is educating consumers on the practical applications of social media networks, such as Facebook, Twitter, LinkedIn, **and** YouTube as well as apps.

As a recognized authority on social media, she has appeared in *The Huffington Post, Entrepreneur Magazine, Glamour Magazine, Bloomberg Business Week,* and in *The Associated Press*. She was the past expert on a weekly technology segment on Houston's Fox television affiliate.

Crystal is the author of the book *The Social Media Why: A Busy Professional's Practical Guide to Using Social Media Including LinkedIn, Facebook, Twitter, YouTube, Pinterest, Google+ and Blogs for Business.*

CPSIA information can be obtained
at www.ICGtesting.com
Printed in the USA
BVOW09s1141280717

490453BV00007B/54/P